Praise for THE
MYSTERY
OF IT ALL

"To read the never prosaic, always poetic, prose of Paul Mariani's *The Mystery of It All* is to feel called to action and then guided by a voice at once both lovingly personal and yet passionately prophetic, the voice of not just an intellectual but also a spiritual father. Readers, writers, teachers, and editors of literature informed by the Catholic intellectual tradition will find some of the most beautiful passages from centuries of great works of literature—that Mariani reminds us have become 'fragments shored against . . . ruins' and wants us to 'piece together' into 'a complex, exciting, reworked, and re-vivifying mosaic,' remembering to preserve 'that sense of awe and wonder' in the presence of the 'incomprehensible certainty' of the Mystery that 'continues to beckon and burn.'"
　　　　—MARY ANN B. MILLER, professor of English, Caldwell University;
　　　　　　　founding editor, *Presence: A Journal of Catholic Poetry*

"A profound *tour de force*, combining the passions of a great and generous literary mind with the self-interrogations of a pilgrim. I have long admired Paul Mariani's extraordinary ability to engage and empathetically enter the interior lives of the poets he studies; his accomplishment and capacious scope is exemplary of what we have come to call the Catholic imagination, an imagination that demonstrates how each substantive voice serves to continue and to enhance the essential utterances of many."
　　　　—SCOTT CAIRNS, author of *Slow Pilgrim: The Collected Poems*
　　　　　　　and *Anaphora: New Poems*

"Acclaimed as a biographer and poet, Paul Mariani is also revered as an exciting, learned, passionate teacher. There's no better place to get a sense of those combined talents than in this wonderful collection of essays."
　　　　—RON HANSEN, author of *Mariette in Ecstasy* and *Atticus*

"

THE MYSTERY OF IT ALL

The Vocation of Poetry in the Twilight of Modernity

PAUL MARIANI

PARACLETE PRESS
BREWSTER, MASSACHUSETTS

2019 First Printing

The Mystery of It All: The Vocation of Poetry in the Twilight of Modernity

Copyright © 2019 by Paul Mariani

ISBN 978-1-64060-333-2

Library of Congress Cataloging-in-Publication Data

Names: Mariani, Paul L., author.
Title: The mystery of it all : the vocation of poetry in the twilight of
    modernity / Paul Mariani.
Description: Brewster, Massachusetts : Paraclete Press, [2019]
Identifiers: LCCN 2019020729 | ISBN 9781640603332 (tradepaper)
Subjects: LCSH: Religious poetry, American--History and criticism. |
    Christian poetry, American--History and criticism. | Christianity and
    literature--United States--History. | Catholics--United
    States--Intellectual life. | Modernism (Literature)--United States.
Classification: LCC PS310.R4 M37 2019 | DDC 811.009/3823--dc23
LC record available at https://lccn.loc.gov/2019020729

10 9 8 7 6 5 4 3 2 1

Published by Paraclete Press
Brewster, Massachusetts
www.paracletepress.com

Printed in the United States of America

FOR EILEEN

Moon, old moon, dear moon, I beg you

answer me when I call out to you,

as I have from the eerie hospital bed,

or over the lit dashboard of my car, or from

the north room where my love is sleeping now,

here next to me, as she has for fifty years

and more, constant companion, ancient

moon, as we go silvering on, alleluia.

CONTENTS

The poem of the mind in the act of finding
What will suffice.
. . . It has to be living, to learn the speech of the place.
It has to face the men of the time and to meet
The women of the time. It has to think about war
And it has to find what will suffice.

     WALLACE STEVENS, "Of Modern Poetry"[1]

————

Oh how I wished to see our image fuse
With the Divine Circle and find its place in it,

But my own wings were far too weak for that.
And then, like that, my mind was struck by lightning,
And with this light received what it had asked.

Here words failed my high imagination.
But by now my desire and will were already
Moving, like a wheel revolving uniformly

By the Love that moves the sun and other stars.

    DANTE, *Paradiso*, c. XXXIII[2]

L ike others, I have spent the better part of my life in pursuit of words that might answer my deepest longings for self-realization. And now, as I approach eighty and watch my friends dying or winding up in hospitals and hospices, I ask myself, once again: Am I any closer to a final resolution? There are moments when I lie in bed in the dark, my CPAP strapped to my face, trying to pray for clarity as I wait to drift off once more, wondering if I will awake tomorrow morning, and—if I do—what then? Where do I pick up and continue?

Because I think of myself as a wordsmith, the way my father thought of himself as a mechanic, and because I have only one good ear and so have always had to pay more attention to words than many, words have always been foremost for me, especially words that signify, that chime, that somehow capture a glimmer of something within or below or above the quotidian. Something that satisfies, if even for a moment, what William Carlos Williams called a kind of grasshopper transcendence. Up, up, and then down again, back to the world around us. It's a transcendence that at best reveals itself in a passing moment— sometimes startling me, but more often something that comforts, as if it said, *see, I am here, I was here*, before it moves on, like the sun breaking through rainclouds for a moment only to transform the trees and the river, before the gray clouds take possession once more.

Music has done this for me—from plainsong to choral to those old Scottish ballads, or from Handel and Mozart and Beethoven and Chopin to Bessie Smith and Bob Dylan and Aretha Franklin. So too with art, from Byzantine icons and mosaics to Giotto's frescoes and Fra Angelico to Botticelli, and on from da Vinci and Breughel and Rembrandt to Cézanne and Renoir and Degas, as well as Picasso and Cassatt and Klimt to Marsden Hartley and Jackson Pollack.

But it is poetry I keep coming back to, which is the reason I spent so many years teaching all sorts of poetry classes, from the lyric to the epic, as well as writing biographies of six of the poets who touched me so deeply: Hopkins and Stevens and Williams, as well as Hart Crane and Berryman and Lowell. The truth is there are so many poets and writers I have admired—dozens and dozens of them: French, Italian, German, Spanish, and Latin American, above all. But particularly poets writing in the English language from the author of Beowulf to Langland and Chaucer and Shakespeare and the Metaphysical poets. And then there are the Irish poets—Yeats and Seamus Heaney especially—as well as Canadian, African, and Australian poets.

But it's to American poetry I keep returning, from Bradstreet and Taylor and on to those two giants, Whitman and Dickinson, as well as the Modernists and poets of the Harlem Renaissance. Because that's who and what I am: someone who grew up in New York City and environs (including northern New Jersey and Long Island), raised as a Catholic by a Catholic father and a self-effacing, wonderful, non-practicing Lutheran mother, whose Polish-Catholic father died in his mid-thirties as a result of the effects of mustard gas contacted during the last stages of World War I, raised by her plucky, self-determined Swedish-American mother.

All this, of course, is another story.

The main thing here is this: early on, I felt touched by Christ's presence, touched so deeply that I cannot think of life now without him nor do I want to, for where else would I turn? Sometimes I have a glimpse of Christ as I walk behind him. True, all I can make out is his long, dark hair and his strong shoulders covered by a plain beige-white workman's cloak as he keeps walking ahead.

And then the image is gone again.

But somehow that presence is enough. Come, he seems to keep saying. Follow me. And I follow behind, sometimes striding, sometimes hobbling, as I try to keep up. There are all kinds of dangers out there, he seems to be telling me, but somehow his presence is enough. He's like one of those Army lieutenants you learn to trust because he's leading from the front and not behind as we move toward one more war zone. And of course there have been many times where I have been blessed to rest with him in some field or at some table filled with good things to eat. It's been like that, really, since I was a boy living on New York's East 51st Street, when my father was in the army during World War II, and all these years later, years I sometimes thought I would never live to see. It's like that still.

Maybe it was the readings from the Old and New Testaments, including the Psalms, that poured over me each Sunday and Holy Day at Mass, then and later, when I was an altar boy answering the priest's *Introibo ad altare Dei* with my own *Ad Deum qui lætificat iuventútem meam* (*I will go up to the altar of God. To God who gives joy to my youth*, from Psalm 43). The joy of my youth, indeed: the privilege of riding my bike through the deserted streets of Levittown to get to the old hangar converted to St. Bernard's Church, then to don that black chasuble and white surplice, and attend the priest at morning Mass, while a handful of the faithful knelt in the pews behind me.

That, and the language of comic books, the New York idiom of Fiorello LaGuardia's forties: Superman, Batman, the Green Lantern, the Katzenjammer Kids, Li'l Abner. In short, my introduction to the American idiom. And by the time I was a teenager, I was beginning to look for poems that could somehow sustain me: poems I could believe in, words I could rely on and believe in, poems in the *ta-dum ta-dum ta-dum* of rhymed iambic pentameter lines, though I didn't quite understand what that meant then. This of course was before I ever thought of picking up the challenge of writing poetry myself.

But what kind of poetry?

I love poems. All kinds of poems. And when I read something that touches me, I want to go deeper, probe further, go beyond the text to the human being who wrote those lines, and even try to discover why such and such a poet wrote the way he or she did. Early on, when it was not the critically popular way to do things, I wanted to get to the psychogenesis of the thing, to the man or woman who wrote those lines and try to understand what the personal and historical pressures on the poet were: the grit and sand that the poet somehow turned into a pearl of lasting, resonant beauty.

In time I came to appreciate the poetry of my beloved Dante and Langland and Chaucer and Shakespeare and the Metaphysical poets, especially that beautiful soul George Herbert. In time too I came to admire Milton and Dryden and Pope and Johnson and the Romantics, especially Keats.

But it was Hopkins who changed everything for me, because, as much as I admired Thompson and Yeats and T. S. Eliot and Pound, in Hopkins I found a kindred soul: a poet of the first order, someone for whom his faith was a living flame. I was twenty-two when I made that discovery in a class I took with Dr. Paul Cortissoz in my senior year at Manhattan College, and that, I now see in hindsight, changed everything for me. Here was a poet for whom a Catholic (Anglo first, and then Roman) and, more specifically, Jesuit framework informed—no, transformed—not only his lines but his very life.

There are many fascinating and truly viable voices out there, and I have learned much from them over the years, as I do to this day. But three have resonated most profoundly with me. One is Dante in his *Divine Comedy*. Another is Flannery O'Connor in her stories and letters. And the third is Hopkins. So much so that I wrote my dissertation on the poet, and I still remember how I recited "The Wreck of the Deutschland" to my infant son Paul as I rocked him in his cradle with my foot and he stared back at me, gurgling his response. Is it any wonder that in time he should become a Jesuit priest himself?

This is why, following the programmatic introductory chapter devoted to the vocation of the Catholic poet today, nearly half of the following pages, constituting the first section, explore various aspects of Hopkins's poetry and the impact it has had on the poetry of the last hundred years, beginning with the posthumous publication of his work by Robert Bridges in 1918. If he published virtually nothing in his own lifetime, the influence Hopkins has had since then, beginning especially with poets like Hart Crane and W. H. Auden, as well as Lowell, Bishop, and Berryman and continuing unabated up to the present, has more than made up for that initial vacuum.

What follows in the second section are chapters, many of them published in magazines and journals in earlier forms over the past two decades, devoted to the impact other poets have had on my understanding of the scintillant in the ordinary, particularly Wallace Stevens, William Carlos Williams, and John Berryman. Each has added splendidly to the available stock of poetic reality, given their wit, humor, and precision, both formal and abstract: all things indispensable to successful poetry.

The essays in the third and final section represent some of the work I have done on the Catholic Imagination during my sixteen years at Boston College, first writing for *Boston College Magazine*, edited by Ben Birnbaum, as well as serving for several years as panelist and contributor for the Boston College Roundtable's *Advancing the Mission of Catholic Higher Education*. And then there's my work with *America* magazine, where I served as poetry editor for six years, as well as my contributions over the past twenty-five years to Greg Wolfe's *Image* journal. There's much more, but let these serve for these pages, which I see as a continuation of the critical work I published back in 1984 under the title *A Usable Past*, followed by a second volume, *God & the Imagination*, in 2002.

Given the nature of things, and given that the shadows continue to lengthen, this volume is an attempt to sum up my continued preoccupation with the sacramental possibilities of the poetic, which begins (and ends) with the question of the vocation of the Catholic poet in our time, a time as fluid as any other, but with its own distinctive characteristics, including the abiding, pressing problematic of a Catholic poet trying to write poetry in what we all recognize as the twilight of modernity. This theme, finally, occupies my thoughts in the book's epilogue as I look forward to a yet unknown future, musing on what remains to be done by those who will take up the call of the Catholic poet in years to come.

THE VOCATION OF THE CATHOLIC POET TODAY

B oston College. I'm sitting in on a meeting of our English Department, the senior faculty, twenty of us, and we're going over some of the future directions our department will be taking. The discussion ebbs and flows, flows and ebbs, some speaking more pointedly and eloquently than others about the merits of this and that: of transnationalism, film studies, American studies, cultural studies, the effects of East/West connections and hybridizations in popular films coming out of Hollywood and Bollywood. For a moment attention shifts to films portraying Victorian characters in minor classics I realize I have never read and probably never will. Someone mentions Indian versions of African hip-hop, another speaks of eighteenth-century wax dolls and effigies of dead children done in beeswax and dressed in crinoline, of the long tradition of what she refers to as Catholic idolatry figured in statues of Mary and a panoply of saints.

I drift back now to other such meetings, forty years of them—at places like Colgate, Hunter, John Jay, and especially the University of Massachusetts/Amherst, where I taught for thirty-two years. The hot topics evoked there and then over the years were the Canon and the

New Canon and the anti-Canon, the New Feminism, African American studies, Native American studies, Irish studies, Holocaust studies, Nuyorican studies, Structuralism and Post-Structuralism, the Gothic and the Neo-Gothic, folklore studies, the literature of the various New Diasporas coming out of South America, Korea, Japan, India, China, and the Philippines, each and every one proposed with a burning zeal as the next wave of concern and interest, only the faces of the proponents shifting or aging or disappearing with the passage of the years.

And so it has gone on, in the great going round of things, all voices worthy to be heard, paid attention to, heeded. But for me, raised in the great tradition of Catholic and Reformation thought and the classics—Hellenism and Hebraism combined and expanded—something central, something on which to hang everything else, seems missing. And suddenly it occurs to me again what that bracing presence Flannery O'Connor once said, that "you have to push as hard as the age that pushes against you." She was speaking of the inherent skepticism of the Catholic scholar of one candle, small as that light may appear to be, facing this new idea and that interminably, *per saecula et saeculorum*, world without end. Then as now, now as then.

The mind wanders, goes back fifty years to 1958 and a young man of eighteen about to graduate from high school. I'm sitting in a small dark antechamber somewhere on the campus of Manhattan College in the Bronx, two hundred yards from the last stop on the elevated IRT, listening to a Christian brother in black soutane and a white collar that sticks out like the tablets Moses brought down from Sinai done in miniature, as he explains to me Manhattan's core program in the liberal arts, a program somehow brought over to the Bronx from Hellas and Rome and Paris and London, a program for young men whose fathers drive trucks or deliver mail or sell insurance or run gas stations or work in offices in Manhattan or one of the boroughs, or are small-town doctors somewhere in the suburbs, or who make their living as cops and firemen on the borough beats. The program in the humanities will be a small group of young men, he explains, for those interested in history and philosophy and literature and art and music and theology, small because most students at Manhattan are bent on becoming successful engineers and businessmen.

Here is what we will learn, Brother explains. We will study ancient cultures—Egyptian and Assyrian, Babylonian and Persian, Hebrew and Greek, Roman and North African to begin with. We will read Homer, Aeschylus, Sophocles, and Euripides, then move on to Hesiod and Sappho and the pre-Socratics, followed by Plato and Aristotle. Then on to Menander and Horace and Virgil, Suetonius, Caesar and Cicero and Catullus, then Livy, Pliny, and Petronius. We will study the Four Evangelists—the Rebel, the Rabbi, the Commentator, and the Mystic—in the light of Genesis and Kings and Ezekiel and Isaiah and Job and the Minor Prophets, as well as the book of Revelation in light of the book of Daniel. We will study St. Paul as he fans out from Antioch and Jerusalem into Galatia and Philippi and Corinth and Ephesus and—finally—Rome. At the core of it all, dividing BC from AD—or BCE from CE—will be the unspoken assumption of the Logos, the radical idea of Incarnation, God's entering the stage of history in a long-forgotten village seven miles southwest of Jerusalem called Bethlehem.

All of this, he tells me and the others in the room, will occur in my first year alone, when I will have to make the daily trek from Mineola to Riverdale and back while working nights—six to eleven—in the local A&P. I can still remember my head soaring and singing on the subway ride home, as the treasure box of World Culture for a moment opened, all that gold glimmering against the shadows. It was like some truly brave new world, this: a new freedom, something greater even than working in my father's Sinclair gas station, something more sustaining even than the conversations one listened to in Ringen's Drugstore over a Coke, or even in the Colonial Bar and Grill, when I was finally old enough to enter through those hallowed swinging doors into the inner temple and order a beer.

Different too from what the radio bleated, or what went on for the most part on the small sea-greenish black and white television in our living room, or the conversations we engaged in each long winter's night to pass the time as we stacked the shelves at the local A&P with peas and pears and pasta under the watchful eye of Big Artie. It would be, poring over these texts preserved over the centuries and delivered to us now in cheap paperbacks, like entering through the granite portals fronting us into a brand new heavenly greensward with stately maples, while the swirling world ground on as it did then and does now each day, just beyond the world of books.

I don't know how many of my fellow students shared the same enthusiasm for all this new learning that I did. In some instances I think yes, as with my classmate John Monahan, who picked me up and drove me to school each day. With others, there was far less enthusiasm. But for me, this opportunity to learn came as nothing less than a birthright, being offered to me thirty miles from the modest home I shared with my parents and six other siblings on Colonial Avenue in Mineola, Long Island.

Two years earlier, I'd entered Marianist Prep, a high school for boys trying to discern whether they had a vocation to this brotherhood of teachers. I'd spent three years at prestigious Chaminade High and, after a young, idealistic priest had called me in to confer with him about whether I might have a vocation, I decided to see for myself. I did discern—discerned something—but not what I had expected. At the beginning of September 1956, my father had driven my mother and me up to Beacon, New York, in the family's '49 two-tone green-on-green Pontiac. On a late summer's day, we made our way up Route 9, at times in sight of the still-majestic if polluted Hudson River, where, after a hug and a handshake, I was deposited to begin my life as a novice in an unimaginable new world.

The school itself—or rather the building that served as both dormitory and classroom space—sat on an old estate surrounded by maples and birches and oaks. Vast open fields ran downhill, facing toward the ancient wooden tram that ascended Mount Beacon, its summit often lost in a swirl of clouds like some latter-day Jacob's ladder ascending Mount Tabor. Each day, along with some forty other young men, I prayed the Mass in Latin in the small, intimate chapel with its tiny white neo-Gothic altar, or played football and baseball under the stately maples, or tobogganed down hills in the pristine silence of new-fallen snow.

I read Virgil in my faltering Latin, learned about the KKK and the Communist Party and the FBI, worked in the antiquated room that stood in for our physics lab, and—as resident artist—painted huge watercolor murals for Halloween and Christmas. I tried to make political sense out of the flickering images on the small television in the common room of a man named Fidel Castro hiding out in the hills of eastern Cuba and attacking Batista's police stations, or pored over images pinned up on the bulletin board from Life magazine of the bodies of Russian NKVD officers on the cobbled streets of Budapest, their grisly uniformed bodies coated with quicklime.

Somehow all these fragments, these shards of news that, Heraclitean-like, kept shape-shifting, I tried to piece together around what for me and the others there constituted the central reality of the Incarnation. If God did enter the world of time and space in the figure of Jesus of Nazareth, then didn't that radically shift the unfolding drama of existence? That event—of God entering our world physically—would make everything count, because it meant that humans on our tiny planet, somewhere in the middle of one galaxy among the countless many, counted, actually mattered, with the verbal pun intended, in the infinite mind of God. That we were not finally random figures in a random universe, but that there was a design in all of this that our human reason could confirm in part, and that the human heart might then assent to.

For if the Incarnation was real, then the possibility that the Creator cared for us, incredible as it seems, cared enough to give his broken sons and daughters His Son, the One who would take on our burdens, empty

Himself of His Godhead, and—as Annie Dillard once phrased it—lift us with Himself when he entered into the presence of the Father again. Therefore the reenactment of the Last Supper in the daily sacrifice of the Mass was all-important: a way of returning to Christ in the Last Supper, itself a reenactment of the Passover meal, on the night that the Son was betrayed by one of his own—as the Mass reminds us—when Christ took unleavened bread and a cup of wine and told his followers that this was how he would remain with them, that this bread and this wine were indeed the real presence of his body and his blood to be shared with each of us in a scene reenacted each day around the world—whether in New York or Newark or Turners Falls or Missoula or Shanghai or Casablanca, as in ancient Rome and Jerusalem and Antioch and Corinth, wherever two or more gathered in community over the past two thousand years.

Beacon, that aptly named town, is where I more fully came to love study, to love words and respect ideas and hunger after knowledge in a way I knew even then would stay with me for the rest of my life. I spent a year among these blessed hills, and then returned home, and—after some anguishing—decided not to enter the novitiate proper. I remember one afternoon on the soccer field at Beacon Prep, serving as goalie as the action went on down at the other goal for a moment, daydreaming about a cheerleader whom I had evoked out of thin air, deciding there and then that, if I left the priesthood and got married and had a family, I would carry on in the best way I could of what had been given me. It is a promise that I have renewed many times to myself over the ensuing half century, and that I mean to keep honoring until the final bell tolls for me.

Fast-forward a dozen years. It's 1970. I'm thirty now, married to my dear wife, and the father of three sons. I have a fresh PhD, and I'm teaching at the University of Massachusetts as a new assistant professor of English. I've driven down to meet a hall full of cadets at West Point on the Hudson to give a talk on the devolving trope of birds in poetry— from Shelley's Skylark to Hopkins's Windhover to Hardy's Darkling

Thrush and on through Ted Hughes's terrifying Crow, before getting back into my Ford and driving home. On the way north, I stop off in Beacon to see how the old school is doing, only to discover that it's . . . now gone. Gone the classrooms and gone the dining hall where the little order of German nuns fed us. Gone, too, the chapel. In its place rises a new brick public high school building big enough to hold hundreds of young men and women. In the years between, while I was busy doing other things, a way of life vanished, almost—by the looks of things—as if it had never been. Footfalls down the long paths, leading into the quiet chapel with its wooden pews and ornate tabernacle housing the Lord: gone, all gone, except in the flickering memory.

Fast-forward another thirty-eight years, and I'm standing in an auditorium in Missoula, Montana, on an evening in late October to talk about something called "the Catholic Intellectual and the Writer," and of the intervening fifty years of trying to recover for others what has stayed with me as it has, in various protean guises, with others: a treasure house of still-vital traditions that seems too often to have been either neglected, covered over with the sands of time, or—to shift the image—plowed under, leaving only golden glitters here and there: fragments shored against one's ruins to be pieced together, one can only hope, once more into a complex, exciting, reworked, and revivifying mosaic.

It's as if one were to take the brilliant shards available to those who are interested and to make of these things—or better, perhaps to discover there—something new, which is the work, after all, of each generation as it searches the ground upon which it walks for what is still useful. I think of young Robert Lowell, still burning with the first flush of his conversion to the Catholic faith, raiding the Scholastic treasury for theological terms he could bring to bear on the critical reading of contemporary literature. At twenty-five, he had pored over Hopkins's Terrible Sonnets and "The Wreck of the Deutschland," until their theological insights had found their way into the language and vision of his own religious ode, "The Quaker Graveyard in Nantucket," which is as much about the moral costs of America pursuing a policy of murderous innocence in fighting evil as it is an elegy to his cousin Warren Winslow, who died when his ship exploded off the coast of New Jersey during World War II. Lowell saw, too, that while Hopkins's new-sprung rhythm, which gave a dramatic new reading to poetry, was important, it was also a part of Hopkins's deeper theological reading of inscape and instress in the very nature of language. What fascinated Hopkins and Lowell—and in turn me—was nothing less than a renewed and energized language that could provide a deeper way of seeing into the nature of reality, including the social, moral, and even political reality underlying history.

So it is with what Catholic theology understands as the sacramental reality of things, a looking further and deeper into the nature and interconnectedness of things, with the belief, perhaps the understanding, that what at first seems random is in fact connected at some very deep cosmological, molecular, and spiritual level: that life is sacred, and that things and events and people do matter, though we may not always understand how. In this tradition there is a long and time-honored list of Catholic writers who also matter—from the church fathers to Augustine and Albertus Magnus and the Victorines, to Dante and Chaucer and Shakespeare and Donne and Herbert and Crashaw and Francis of Assisi and John of the Cross and Catherine of Siena and Teresa of Ávila and Villon and Dostoyevsky—and so on, through to John Henry Newman and Gerard Manley Hopkins and Hillaire Belloc and G. K. Chesterton and George Bernanos and T. S. Eliot, and—closer to our own time—the figures of Dorothy Day, Flannery O'Connor, Thomas Merton, Wallace Stevens, Walker Percy, Annie Dillard, Denise Levertov, Mary Gordon, Alice McDermott, Mary Karr, Franz Wright, and Ron Hansen, to speak only of Western literature.

I'm aware, especially in my roles as biographer, critic, and poet, that the area of expertise I can lay even tentative claim to is pitiably small. But I am also aware of a huge, interlocking world of others who also share my concern for the sacramental aspects of nature, as well as of the problematics of intrinsic good and evil, the search for meaning, and more, the search for God in all of this. To be a Christian writer means doing what any writer worthy of the name must do: it means reading continually and continually assessing what you read. But add to this the idea of Catholic, as Flannery O'Connor pointed out years ago, which means—in the grand economy of time—understanding the importance of prayer and the real presence in the Eucharist. For if the Eucharist were only a symbol, she once told Mary McCarthy and Robert Lowell over dinner, then the hell with it.

It also means listening hard for the truth amid a veritable deluge of language and of what passes for knowledge, or, if not knowledge, then information. It means looking hard at things until you are at last convinced that they have revealed a glimmer of the phosphorescent truth they so often seem to cover and contain within themselves. O'Connor for one spoke of her Catholic skepticism as a way of holding on to what was most dear to her. Which means holding back from the mesmeric claims of advertising or the demands of the media or the internet on one's attention: of being wary of the smoothest rhetoric, where one is urged to agree with the majority, even though something in oneself holds back.

We know that to say yes to something, to give oneself over to it, can be a dangerous thing, though—paradoxically—it is a gesture that can also radically free the self. So with the act of writing poetry, something that has taken me in directions I had never thought to go. I began writing poems forty years ago, when I was in my mid-thirties, just after my Pop-Pop, my mother's mother, died from the effects of alcoholism. I loved the woman, mind you, for she had often served as a guardian angel for me, and I wanted to honor her memory, to hold in words and music something of that resilient spirit of hers that had—against the odds—weathered so much pain and disappointment before death came calling and knocked on her apartment door.

I remember sitting at my brother's dining room table down in Baldwin, Long Island, getting ready to go to my grandmother's funeral, and trying to understand why I had wept so furiously at the wake the night before. To try to understand, I found myself staring at a blank piece of paper and a pen and then writing a draft of "Emely," a poem that opens with a boy of seven sitting at a kitchen table in a dark fifth-floor tenement building on Manhattan's Fifty-Third Street, between First and Second Avenue, a Civil War brownstone long torn down to be replaced by something more chic and modern. On the "scratched tintop table," she had "spread out / a feast of sweet jam"—a jar of A&P cherry jam, I remember—as she questioned me on how my parents' troubled marriage was faring. "That dark tenement," I began, using William Carlos Williams's late stepdown triplet lines, a poet I was obsessed with even then:

> That dark tenement that
> smelled of kerosene is
> gone, like you. On
>
> the scratched tintop
> table you have spread out
> a feast of sweet
>
> jam and milky tea to ply me
> with, to find out how
> my father treats
>
> your daughter. It shakes me
> that you know my secret. . . .[3]

When I wrote those lines—back in 1974, half a lifetime ago—my parents were in the process of divorcing after thirty-five years of marriage and seven children. Somehow—somehow—the words on the page I wrote that morning brought with them a certain comfort and even unexpected joy that, though something had been lost, something had also been recovered in the music of those lines.

Such was the beginning of my serious pursuit of poetry. Not the study of it; that I had been doing for a dozen years by then, but the writing itself. In some sense I could follow, at a distance, those poets and thinkers whom I so cherished, whether Hopkins or Eliot or Pound or Hart Crane or Stevens or—in this case—using the three-part step-down line I'd learned from William Carlos Williams. I would go on to write biographies of five poets and shards of others—first Williams, then Berryman, then Lowell, then Hart Crane, then the poet closest to my own heart, Fr. Hopkins, and, finally, Stevens, the poet I have read and taught for the past half century and more.

But there was something else that came with writing poetry. And that had to do with the necessity of growing into the person who could write the poems I wanted to write. Once, back in the late 1970s, sitting in a pub in Amherst, Massachusetts, with the Irish poet John Montague, I showed him one of my poems about being a father to three sons. He looked it over, nodded, then handed it back to me. Eleven years my senior, he too wanted to write about what it meant to be a father, he confessed, but first he would have to grow into the man and poet who could do that.

It is that sense of growing into the poet you eventually hope to be, a hope that will always be only partially realized as you keep trying to move in the direction of that elusive, haunting figure of the self, knowing in the case of the writer for whom the spiritual dimension must be accounted for, that you have been preceded by Flannery O'Connor and T. S. Eliot and Gerard Manley Hopkins and John of the Cross and Dante. Especially Dante. Consider the following lines, which owe much to my good fortune in having had Allen Mandelbaum, Dante scholar, translator, and poet, as my mentor. It's called "Silt," and I wrote it after suffering a deep vein thrombosis just weeks after taking a new teaching

position at Boston College at the age of sixty and driving the ninety
miles to teach classes, before returning home again. "How it steals up
on you," the poem begins,

> this mortality,
> dropping its calling card, say, after the flight
> back from your friend's wedding, six kinds of wine
> on a stone veranda overlooking the starlit sea
>
> while migrants labor in the fields beneath.
> One morning you bend down to lace
> your sneakers and find your leg stiff as a base-
> ball bat. How many times you told yourself Death
>
> wouldn't catch you unaware, the way, alas,
> it did so many of your friends. That you'd hie
> yourself off to the hospital at the first sign
> of trouble. And then, when it should happen, as
>
> it has, you go into denial once again, while your
> poor leg whimpers for attention, until at last you get
> the doctor, who finds a fourteen-inch blood clot
> silting up your veins there on the sonar.
>
> Mortality's the sticking thinners twice
> each day into your stomach, until the skin screams
> a preternatural black and blue. Mortality's
> swallowing the stuff they use to hemorrhage mice.
>
> It's botched blood tests for months on end.
> Admit it, what's more boring than listening to
> Another's troubles, except thumbing through
> postcards of others on vacation. Friendly Finland,

Warsaw in July. Mortality's my leg, her arm, your heart.
Besides, who gives a damn about the plight of others
except the saints and God? But isn't death the mother
of us all? Shouldn't death mean caring, the moving out

at last beyond the narrow self? But who has
time for that? Six wines on a stone veranda,
stars, a summer moon high over Santa Monica,
cigars from verboten old Havana, live jazz.

That's what one wants. That, and not some blood
clot clogging up one's veins. No poet will ever
touch again what Dante somehow touched there
at the *Paradiso*'s end. It was there he had St. Bernard

beseech his Lady to look upon him that she might
grant him light and understanding, which he might
share in turn with others. Lady, cast thine eyes,
I pray thee, down towards me. I cannot take much height,

though God knows I've tried. Six wines, two cigars,
a summer moon over the veranda, where I kept tilting
outwards, my veins absorbing even then the *gravitas* of silting
while Love was busy moving the sun and other stars.[4]

L'amor che move il sole e l'altre stelle: perhaps the times are unpropitious for
striving after a vision like Dante's, who had the help of Giotto and Fra
Angelico with his smiling angels and Albertus Magnus and John Duns
Scotus and Thomas Aquinas and the Dominicans and the Franciscans
for moral support. Perhaps. But isn't it exciting to think in those terms,
to think that one might use that template rather than those others one

has been urged to endorse in our time? Certainly, Eliot understood this, which is why he kept a copy of Dante in his coat pocket and read from him each lunch time at Lloyds of London, where he clerked. If we are what we eat, then how much more are we what we read, watch, or listen to. It takes a lifetime to realize who we are, as even Dante learned, working step by step down through the depths of his Inferno before rising into his Purgatory and eventually into the glimpsed vision of Paradise above, all the while exiled from his beloved Florence, always climbing a stranger's stairs, his mind and spirit growing clearer and bolder and more luminous with each ascending step. But not without its cost. Assuredly not without its cost.

All along the way, you come to learn, you must write from where you are, arriving at a place you did not know and see it for the first time. Allen Mandelbaum, sitting in the main study of the artist Leonard Baskin's home in Northampton, Massachusetts, myself a young assistant professor just starting out, listening to Baskin excoriate Eliot for his anti-Semitism, and Allen responding. Yes, yes, but then there were these lines by Eliot to consider, which seemed to sum up his own efforts over the years. And then, from memory, he proceeds to quote the lines I have put down here: "So here I am," Eliot confessed in *East Coker*, the words remaining with me even now:

> So here I am, in the middle way, having had twenty years—
> Twenty years largely wasted, the years of *l'entre deux guerres*—
> Trying to learn to use words, and every attempt
> Is a wholly new start, and a different kind of failure
> Because one has only learnt to get the better of words
> For the thing one no longer has to say, or the way in which
> One is no longer disposed to say it. And so each venture
> Is a new beginning, a raid on the inarticulate
> With shabby equipment always deteriorating
> In the general mess of imprecision of feeling,

Undisciplined squads of emotion. And what there is to conquer
By strength and submission, has already been discovered
Once or twice, or several times, by men whom one cannot hope
To emulate—but there is no competition—
There is only the fight to recover what has been lost
And found and lost again and again. . . .[5]

One writes, one thinks, one listens hard, one pushes back (Flannery O'Connor again) where one has to, all the while remaining open to new possibilities, to the fact that the Mystery of God speaks in its own language, in a language that is wordless, though we know too well we need words to try to understand, to use the best ones we can come up with, though all words, however much they may add to the available stock of reality, must finally crack, slip, slide, recover themselves beneath the void, and ultimately, it seems, disappoint.

There's a story from the Acts of the Apostles that has stayed with me, one that acts as a sober reminder of the paradox that is at the heart of speaking of the self as a Catholic or Christian or as an intellectual. Sometime around the year 52, the apostle Paul—moving down from Macedonia through Thessalonica and Boroea on his second mission—arrived in Athens, where he commenced preaching, first to his fellow Jews in the local synagogue, and then in the central marketplace, the Agora. It was there that he met the philosophers of the day: Stoics and Epicureans, men, Luke tells us in the Acts of the Apostles, who loved to argue the latest ideas. Some of these philosophers, unlike Socrates certain of their own minds, were put off by Paul, who seemed to keep coming back to a belief in a Nazarene who had risen, he said, from the dead, so that they quickly dismissed him as one who merely parroted the tenets of his sect. Others, however, were intrigued by the originality of what he had to say and invited him to accompany them to the Areopagus, the Sorbonne of their day or the university of our own.

But how to talk about the crucified Christ risen, an idea in its very concept as alien to the Greeks as it was to his fellow Jews? Paul, trained in both Jewish Law and Greek rhetoric, began well enough. On his way up the hill to the Acropolis, he told them, he'd noticed that the polytheistic Greeks, anxious to cover their bets and not overlook some supernatural force they might have inadvertently failed to recognize, had been careful to erect an altar to that Unknown God.

Well, it was this very God, Paul explained, about whom he had come to talk to them. He knew well enough that the group of intellectuals assembled before him did not actually believe in Zeus or Hera or Aphrodite, except as abstract principles or forces or virtues. These were rationalists for the most part, men of the Hellenistic enlightenment, a common-enough ground to be shared by Jew and Greek alike. After all, these were no mere rustics, no hoi polloi, and so he was addressing them accordingly. God had made the world and everything in it, he explained, and so certainly that God did not need to make his home in any shrine, and surely in none of the idols that dotted the streets of Athens or Rome or Ephesus. This same God, or First Principle or Prime Mover, had made the world and everything in it, Paul reiterated, a principle of unity bifurcating and splitting in a kind of Big Bang, Unity becoming Duality in matter. One more version, say, of Bach's *Goldberg Variations*, as it were: Unity, Duality, Trinity, and so forth.

Moreover, this God had created the world and humans, so that the world and its highest apex—creatures gifted with intelligence and self-consciousness—might in turn find their way back to the Creator and First Cause and so discover the face of God in turn. As Paul warmed to his subject, he studded his talk with quotations from the Greek writers with whom his audience would have been familiar, including Aratus the Cilician's *Phainomena*, to the effect that we humans are all God's children. But, alas, in time, the Greeks and the Romans, like the Egyptians and Hittites and Persians and Babylonians and Assyrians before them, had each in their turn gone astray, worshiping not the one God only, but idols, splintering God into an exploding force field of sorts.

Still, God could forgive such ignorance, Paul went on, because now He had come to dwell with humans, having sent his Son into the world to put things right by God's own standards. And this man was Jesus of Nazareth, who had been put to death by the authorities twenty years before and then raised from the dead, a stunning reality witnessed by many, including himself.

Raised from the dead? Someone raised from the dead? When Paul said this, many of the assembled philosophers—tenured and untenured alike, no doubt—began to laugh and mock him. Others more politely suggested that Paul call it a day and come back some other time. Paul, realizing he had been momentarily defeated, left the podium, resolving never again to try and use the lingua franca of the philosophers when attempting to explain a Mystery as profound as the passion, death, and resurrection of his Master. From now on, he realized, another way would have to be found to approach the profound and contradictory sign of the Cross. Talk, however polished, could only take one so far.

It is significant that from Athens Paul went on to Corinth, a seaport town so raucous, vital, and blasphemous that in Paul's time the word *Corinth* had become a popular verb meaning to fornicate. And, he would remind this community when he came to write them two years later, that when he had come, he had come without oratorical brilliance or philosophical wisdom to announce to them nothing less than the wisdom of God.

Not human wisdom, then, but God's wisdom—a "foolishness . . . wiser than human wisdom"—and God's mysterious way of speaking to the world (see 1 Cor. 1:21). "I was resolved," Paul reminded the Corinthians then, "that the only knowledge I would have while I was with you was knowledge of Jesus, and of him as the crucified Christ." And so Paul, having learned his lesson, had addressed them in fear and trembling, proclaiming what he had to say not by philosophical argument, not by thesis and counterthesis, linguistic nicety, or deconstruction, but by trying to "demonstrate the convincing power of the Spirit, so that your faith should depend not on human wisdom but on the power of God."

This is and remains for me the central paradox for the Catholic Christian writer and thinker: that at the heart of the matter is a Mystery so profound that thought alone, language alone, no matter how compelling its force or eloquence or rightness, can never of itself convince us, to say nothing of others. Granted. But I have found that poetry—of all languages—with its metaphor and music and its resonating underthought offers the best way of touching the hearer's heart as well as his or her head. Consider, for example, Fr. Hopkins's short sonnet "Pied Beauty," a poem that is also a paean of praise to that subtle craftsman, God.

"All things therefore are charged with love," Hopkins wrote on one of his spiritual retreats, "are charged with God and *if we know how to touch them* give off sparks and take fire, yield drops and flow, ring and tell of him."[6]

What an extraordinary insight that is, and yet one shared—at least in isolated flecks—by so many of us. Others sense this beauty, but then immediately question it, categorizing it, labeling it, explaining it away, as if it were the wisp end of some waking dream. And so this further paradox: that while we hone our critical and rational and linguistic skills, we have to be reminded from time to time—and in all humility—that, unless we become again as little children, that is, keep that sense of awe and wonder before the Mystery of Creation we had when such things were fresh to us, we cannot enter the realm of heaven. Which I take to mean that, once having decisively cut ourselves off from the Creator, we are left only with brilliant glass shards, a colorful maze, a soup of random protons and neutrons, like Wallace Stevens's speaker standing before the blazing nightfall panorama of the "Auroras of Autumn" in awe and terror.

Hopkins knew what it meant to face the Kantian sublime, the sense of powerlessness before whatever forces sought to overwhelm us—whether the sheer terror of those twin towers collapsing on themselves at the prow of Manhattan, or the scandals that have rocked the Catholic Church and (if the truth be known) many of the churches of our brothers and sisters, or the fear that attends a global market that bangs and tumbles up and down as if its axle were broken. Whatever the nature of the shipwreck, as in his ode to the wrecked steamship the *Deutschland*, it was the sense that, even in that "unshapeable shock night," one might read it aright—like a tall German nun crying out Christ's name in the exploding darkness to come and come quickly to her—and know "the who and the why" beneath the stress: the sense of God's presence in all of this, the conviction that this terrifying darkness was not some random act, but something that went beyond shipwreck, went deeper even than the extremity of chaos unfolding, that all of this was being watched over by a caring God who had, after all, so loved us that he had sent—and was sending us again—His own Son into that same windswept world.

But how come to such a realization of God's underlying presence? And how speak of it convincingly to the world? This is what I mean by saying that the Catholic writer, like any writer, must grow into that voice. It means—as Flannery O'Connor has said—not only doing whatever other writers must do, and doing it well, but in addition intimating something more: that the world means and means deeply, and that, besides order, there is something more: a God who not only shapes but cares for, broods over, yes, loves His Creation and loves us as well, even more than Himself. That, in the midst of a tragedy summed up in the image of shipwreck for Hopkins, whether literally or metaphorically, as he felt when he'd been shipwrecked and abandoned in Ireland. "Across my foundering deck shone / A beacon, an eternal beam," Hopkins wrote from Dublin one afternoon in late July, in the year 1888, ten months before his death.

A beacon. A cross beam gleaming in the darkness of depression. And so he could say, finally: *Enough!* Let "Flesh fade, and mortal trash / Fall to the residuary worm." Yes, let the world's wildfire, the Heraclitean flux of life burn everything in its cosmic bonfire, and let it leave behind ash. No matter, for like St. Paul, he too saw into the mystery of things, that

> In a flash, at a trumpet crash,
> I am all at once what Christ is, since he was what I am, and
> This Jack, joke, poor potsherd, patch, matchwood, immortal diamond,
> Is immortal diamond.

How does one begin to be a poet who could say such a thing, and mean it? That has been my lifetime's struggle, to be achieved, if ever, at the cost of "not less than everything," as T. S. Eliot famously put it in the closing section of his "Little Gidding." Call it the pearl of great price that the Catholic poet, in all humility, knowing the cost, and with failure leering from the grimpens and the fens, keeps slogging after, hoping, drawn on by that same distant beacon, gleaming and beckoning, gleaming and beckoning.

I

ON THE QUIVER
OF MYSTERY

GERARD MANLEY HOPKINS
AND HIS INFLUENCE

1

HOPKINS AND THE
POETICS OF JESUIT SPIRITUALITY

T hou mastering me / God," Hopkins's great ode, "The Wreck of the Deutschland," begins. And there it is, the opening salvo, the overture, as it were, to the young (thirty-one-year-old) Jesuit scholastic's understanding of what he has been sent forth to do. And what is that? Is it not to proclaim the fact that his Lord and Master, Christ, *Ipse*, is—with the Father and the Spirit—worthy of all praise as the Creator whose designs are so often beyond our immediate understanding? And that when those designs are finally glimpsed and somehow understood through patience and prayer, when at last the larger picture begins to reveal itself, we are left with—indeed surprised by—a sense of wonder, awe, and, yes, joy?

It is then that those who have searched in the darkness for an answer as to why there is so much suffering in the world should be consoled beyond anything they might have hoped for, so that they feel blessed, feel so fully realized that only some extravagant gesture—like King David dancing before the ark of the covenant—will do. And so the poet, who kisses his hand toward the night heavens above him, the winter snowstorm having finally lifted and the stars returned now, as if seen for the first time, seeming to wink at him now and to call him home, confesses:

I kiss my hand
To the stars, lovely-asunder
Starlight, wafting him out of it; and
Glow, glory in thunder;
Kiss my hand to the dappled-with-damson west:
Since, tho' he is under the world's splendour and wonder,
His mystery must be instressed, stressed;
For I greet him the days I meet him, and bless when I understand.[7]

It is something Hopkins discerned through living in close community with his fellow Jesuits, through studying and—more—living the day-to-day grind and drudgery of his studies and his work among the poor and marginalized. It is also something he gleaned from the Ignatian *Spiritual Exercises*: that beauty and wonder are not mere accidents caught in the glimmer of light and darkness, but something more, signs of God's presence, the Mystery in and with and through the great design that has always been there, but that has to be instressed upon our minds and—more—upon our hearts. And what is this but the realization that there is a Creator who is also a Father who has loved us so much that he gave us his only Son to bring us home again, so that this reality might become instressed at last upon us, to the point that we have no other choice finally than to greet him, love him, and adore him in return, the way a child runs to embrace a mother, a father.

The *mystery* of it all. And what did Hopkins mean by the word *mystery*? In a letter he wrote in late October 1883 to an old friend, the poet Robert Bridges, raised in an Anglican household, but by then an agnostic, Hopkins explained what he himself meant by mystery. He knew what Bridges no doubt meant when he called the Incarnation a mystery. "You do not mean by mystery what a Catholic does," Hopkins told him, in that bold, no-nonsense way of his when dealing with something as important as the doctrine of the Incarnation.[8] "You mean an interesting [religious] uncertainty," he said, and "the uncertainty ceasing interest ceases also."

But for Catholics—and Jesuits like himself—mystery meant something far greater: "an incomprehensible certainty." Incomprehensible to the human mind, perhaps, but nevertheless something certain, something to be believed in and lived by.

The thing was that there had to be a formulation to the mystery, for without formulation there could be no interest, so that "the clearer the formulation" of the mystery "the greater the interest." For a believer like himself as well as an unbeliever like Bridges, the "source of interest" was the same: "the unknown, the reserve of truth beyond what the mind reaches and still feels to be behind." Yes, Hopkins understood, a religious mystery like the Incarnation or the Trinity might seem to Bridges little more than an intellectual puzzle, a vain curiosity at best, so that, the "curiosity satisfied, the trick found out (to be a little profane), the answer heard," interest in the mystery disappeared.

Not so, on the other hand, for himself. "You know," he continued, how "there are some solutions to . . . . chess problems so beautifully ingenious, some resolutions of suspensions so lovely in music that even the feeling of interest is keenest when they are known and over, and for some time survives the discovery [itself]." But what if the answer to the mystery turned out to be "the most tantalizing statement of the problem," so that the truth one assented to remained by its very nature the great difficulty?

Consider, Hopkins went on, the difference between his mentor, John Henry Cardinal Newman, and Newman's younger brother Francis, who could not assent to the Anglican doctrine required at the time of all Oxford dons, and so had abandoned his studies and left Oxford. If the Trinity, the younger Newman explained, was something that could "be explained by grammar and by tropes, why then he could furnish explanations for himself."[9] And that left the problem of where the real mystery, "the incomprehensible one," finally lay. At that point, Hopkins explained, "one should point blank believe or disbelieve." And so, where the younger brother chose to disbelieve, the older brother came to believe.

That chess move having been made, though, there was something more. For him as a Catholic and a Jesuit, belief in the Trinity was fundamental:

> There are three persons, each God and each the same, the one, the only God: to some people this is a "dogma", a word they almost chew, that is an equation in theology, the dull algebra of Schoolmen; to others it is news of their dearest friend or friends, leaving them all their lives in a balancing whether they have three heavenly friends or one—not that they have any doubt on the subject, but that their knowledge leaves their minds swinging; poised, but on the quiver.

If this was how one should better understand the Trinity, it was likewise true of the vast implications of the Incarnation, a mystery less incomprehensible than the former, perhaps, but for all that no less true. For an unbeliever like Bridges, the Incarnation came down to this: that if Christ was "in some sense God," it was also true that in some sense Christ was *not* God. And therein lay the agnostic's interest: in that puzzling uncertainty. But for Hopkins Christ was "in every sense God and in every sense man," and that was what kept him on and off balance: in the "locked and inseparable combination" of the God-man, Jesus Christ. And that, he explained, was why he, as a Catholic and a Jesuit, spoke of "the mystery of the Nativity" or "the mystery of the Crucifixion": that the infant in the manger was really God, as was "the culprit on the gallows God, and so on." In and of themselves, birth and death are not mysteries, but that God should be crucified for us: *that* was what fascinated him, "with the interest of awe, of pity, of shame, of every harrowing feeling."

Like many who make the Ignatian Long Retreat, Hopkins had thought and thought hard about the reality and endless ramifications of the Mystery of the Incarnation, of Christ's life in Galilee, of the end in the beginning and the beginning foretelling the end: birth to death, Nativity to Passion, and then a birthing into a new life, a new life following death, that divine life growing and blossoming with time, something outside the limits of *chronos*, of human time, something only the heart, like a hart pursued and cornered by baying hounds, would cry out with a final *yes* or *no* that would change everything afterward:

> Warm-laid grave of a womb-life grey;
> Manger, maiden's knee;
>   The dense and the driven Passion, and frightful sweat;
>   Thence the discharge of it, there its swelling to be,
>   Though felt before, though in high flood yet—
> What none would have known of it, only the heart, being hard at bay,
>
>   Is out with it! Oh,
> We lash with the best or worst
>   Word last![10]

To what could he as a poet compare the experience the nuns had undergone as they faced their own imminent end, he asked himself in that winter of 1875, meditating from the relative safety of the fortress-like theologate at St. Beuno's in North Wales when the news broke of the death of those five Franciscan nuns, exiles from their homeland, Germany, all drowned off the coast of England when their ship, the *SS Deutschland*, stranded on a shoal, broke apart? To what compare it? To what experience available to us all? Was it not like biting into a ripe plum, he asked, when the bitterness or sweetness of the crushed fruit fills the mouth and the body to the very brim in a single irreversible instant?

> How a lush-kept plush-capped sloe
> Will, mouthed to flesh-burst,
>   Gush!—flush the man, the being with it, sour or sweet,
>   Brim, in a flash, full!—Hither then, last or first,
>   To hero of Calvary, Christ's feet—
> Never ask if meaning it, wanting it, warned of it—men go.

"Thou mastering me / God": this conviction stands as one of the most important things this young Jesuit in formation understood as he looked back on the spiritual journey he was on, beginning with his family, the oldest child in a large Anglican family of eight siblings, then as an honors student at Oxford, where (to the dismay of his parents) that journey had led to his becoming a Roman Catholic under the guidance of John Henry Newman, who had likewise guided so many other young men at Oxford into or, perhaps, back into the Catholic Church. And then, after further discernment as to whether he should enter the Franciscans or Benedictines, he had decided a year after his conversion and a retreat with the *Exercises* to join the Society of Jesus.

In September 1868, at the age of twenty-four, he underwent the various stages of Jesuit formation, beginning with the novitiate at Roehampton on the southern edge of London, then the Scholasticate at Stonyhurst in the north of England, where he studied philosophy, then a year teaching rhetoric to a class of Jesuits in the early stages of formation. And then it was on to St. Beuno's, where he studied the prescribed curriculum of Scholastic theology in the Thomistic tradition, though while at Stonyhurst he also discovered the writings of the medieval Franciscan friar John Duns Scotus, whose theological treatises he had read in the original Latin.

What Scotus added to the young Jesuit's Romantic sensibility went deeper than an understanding of and appreciation for the generic sense of things, as taught by the Scholastics: the distinctive and individual mark of everything in God's ongoing creation, what Scotus in his own years at Oxford centuries before had called the *haecceitas*—the "thisness"—of each and every created thing. And if Hopkins's particular understanding of God's creation was met with misunderstanding and even suspicion by his professors at St. Beuno's, so was Duns Scotus in his own time and subsequently, for it is from the word Duns that the word *dunce* derives.

But then, as it so often happens, Hopkins understood, Duns Scotus was one of those (not unlike himself, though he did not say so directly) who "saw too far, he knew too much, his subtlety overshot his interests" so that "a kind of feud arose between genius and talent, and the ruck of talent in the Schools finding itself, as his age passed by, less and less able to understand him, voted that there was nothing important to understand and so first misquoted and then refuted him."[11]

But Hopkins read Scotus, as he himself said, with "delight," because Scotus, like Hopkins's senior contemporary John Ruskin, had helped him see the uniqueness and distinctiveness of everything in nature, once it was, in the Jesuit tradition of *contemplatio*, pondered over with prayerful attention. And soon Hopkins was celebrating the pied beauty he was finding everywhere around him in his walks through the Welsh countryside. "I do not think I have ever seen anything more beautiful than the bluebell I have been looking at," he wrote in his journal in May 1870. "I know the beauty of our Lord by it."[12] And it was this sense of the wondrous inscape of a particular thing he caught again seven years later in his condensed sonnet "Pied Beauty," "Glory be to God for dappled things," the poem begins:

> For skies of couple-colour as a brinded cow;
>   For rose-moles all in stipple upon trout that swim;
> Fresh-firecoal chestnut-falls; finches' wings;
>   Landscape plotted and pieced – fold, fallow, and plough;
>   And áll trádes, their gear and tackle and trim.
>
> All things counter, original, spáre, stránge;
>   Whatever is fickle, frecklèd (who knows how?)
>   With swift, slow; sweet, sour; adazzle, dim;
> He fathers-forth whose beauty is past change:
>   Praise him.[13]

Brinded. Couple-colored. Rose-moles. Stippled. Fickle, freckled, adazzle, dim. Look, Hopkins tells us. Behold what is there before you and look at it once more with that original sense of childlike awe and wonder we seem to lose as we grow older and more jaded.

"Man is created to praise, reverence, and serve God our Lord, and by this means to save his soul." Thus the underlying *Principle and Foundation* of the *Spiritual Exercises*. And, Ignatius added, "the other things on the face of the earth are created for man that they may help him in prosecuting the end for which he is created. From this it follows that man is to use them as much as they help him on to his end, and ought to rid himself of them so far as they hinder him as to it." Which I take to mean, God gives us a world of splendor and immensity, and it is our privilege and responsibility as conscious beings to acknowledge that bounty and to praise the Creator for all he has given us.

For Hopkins the Jesuit, God's presence was to be found in everything, however difficult to discern at times, but nevertheless always there: God the Grand Designer and Creator who was beyond change, but who paradoxically underwrites the kaleidoscopic flux that was (and is) the world at each and every moment. It was a world where all things interacted in imitation of the trinitarian three in one—or, as Hopkins rendered this teaching, memorably, the Utterer, the Uttered, and the Uttering, each perpetually reaching out to the Other, who was always also the One.

Consider the ever-changing clouds glimpsed at dawn or dusk, the light changing from minute to minute, or hour by hour, or as rainclouds gather, or high winds begin to blow. Or consider those rose moles stippled brushlike on living trout in the flint-cold streams where Hopkins fished at Stonyhurst and Wales. Note, too, the multifold varieties of color in finches' wings, or those chestnuts that fall and break open to reveal a flame-red center not unlike those chunks of gray-black coal breaking open as they fall through the grating, gashing themselves to reveal at last the fire within.

Is it not like Christ's heart breaking with love and sorrow on the cross, "[t]he dense and the driven Passion, and frightful sweat," and finally "the discharge of it,"[14] the orgasmic bursting of God offering up everything for His rare, dear creation, man? It is something, Hopkins had come to understand, something "none would have known" had it not been instressed on our own hearts: Love itself, nailed to a tree for all to look upon, hands outstretched and pinioned, beckoning, beseeching.

Only in prayerful meditation and something more—a hunger, a need, a cry from the wounded soul—"the heart, being hard at bay"—as when one suddenly realizes that the ship one is on is going down, or when a hart realizes finally that it has been surrounded by baying hounds and that escape is now impossible: it is then that the heart and the words fully confess and are "out with it!" In the cosmic irony of things, then, it is only in Christ's dark descending that he proves "most . . . merciful." And if Hopkins understands this on one level at this point, how much more will he come to understand it eight years on, when he would compose his darkest and richest poems, those terrible and terrifying sonnets written in blood, in which Christ etched—yes, inscaped—his own passion on Hopkins as once he did on Francis of Assisi and Ignatius of Loyola and John of the Cross and Catherine of Siena.

It is that sense of composition of place, not this time meditating as he had in doing the *Exercises*, on the landscapes of Judea and Jerusalem in the reign of the emperor Tiberius, but focusing instead on what the *London Times* had just reported about a shipwreck off the coast of England, where the Thames enters the North Sea. December 6, 1875: a German passenger ship, the *SS Deutschland*, steaming from Bremen, foundered on a strand. For there, in the continual raging of the winter storm, as the ship was knocked about as if by some insane force, the steamer's cabins flooded and the temperatures sinking far below freezing, the ship met with the loss over less than twenty-four hours of a quarter of its two hundred passengers. Among the dead were five Franciscan nuns, exiled by Germany's Second Reich anti-Catholic laws: five women banished from the old and so destined for the new world—New York and St. Louis—to continue their duties serving others.

What was it those five sisters experienced in the midst of that storm, Hopkins asks himself and us? What was it like to wait for help through the darkness and ice and snow when there would be no help forthcoming? What was it like to hear the desperate cries of men and women and children, like so many lost sheep? Or to witness a man attempt to come to the aid of a woman, like some hero out of a Victorian novel to save the day, only to be battered like some plaything against the side of the ship, the headless body looped bizarrely in a sling of ropes, rocking back and forth like some nightmarish pendulum? And when—at last—as the papers reported, the tallest of the five nuns cried out in her agony, "O Christ, Christ, come quickly," what did she mean? Was it a cry of despair to have the agony end? Or was it, rather, that she was calling Christ to her side in this, her final gesture, calling on the only One who could turn "her wild-worst best"?

Often, the Jesuit who wrote these lines understood only too well, when we are exhausted with work—as he would often find himself nodding off under the weight of the hundreds upon hundreds of Greek and Latin exams he meticulously graded winters and summers and in between—a man or a woman will ask for an end to "the jading and jar of the cart," the way some great gray dray horse with its collar strapped about its neck wants nothing more than to lie down exhausted.

Doesn't the appeal of the Passion strike us more tenderly during a thirty-day retreat, say, when one is relatively safe and comfortable indoors as another winter storm comes whipping off the winter ocean? No, it was something else the woman felt then: the sense that Christ was actually with her—*here, and now*—in the midst of the storm. Christ's presence felt, there in the storm, Christ the Paraclete and Comforter: her "Master, / Ipse, the only one, *Chríst, Kíng, Héad*." As at the conclusion of the consecration at the Mass in the Tridentine form of Hopkins's time, when the priest raises the chalice and the host before the congregation of believers and calls out "Per ipsum, et cum ipso, et in ipso, est tibi Deo Patri omnipotenti, in unitate Spiritus

Sancti, omnis honor et gloria per omnia sæcula sæculorum" (Through him, and with him, and in him, O God, almighty Father, in the unity of the Holy Spirit, all honor and glory is yours, forever and ever).

What is the fruit of Hopkins's long meditation on this tragic shipwreck—just one of hundreds one might have read or talked about in a time before air travel, when ships cast off to cross the oceans almost as often as planes taxi off runways today into what only God knows awaits them? Remember, Hopkins tells us, when Christ's hand-picked disciples were out on the Sea of Galilee and one of those sudden squalls came up and the fishing boat they were on seemed in danger of sinking, taking them with it? Remember how they frantically woke Christ, exhausted with having done his Father's work? Remember how they were sure they were perishing then, and how Christ had commanded the very winds to cease and they did, and the waters suddenly calmed?

So now, here, on a December night in the Year of Our Lord 1875, Christ comes to fetch his beloved, to calm her and her sisters and the others—including those "last-breath penitents" awakened by the nun's cry—to gather them as he gathered those souls when he harrowed hell, leading them into an eternal safe haven, beyond reproach or despair. That was what the woman had done by witnessing to her Lord, calling out to him, as now Hopkins likewise does, calling out to those who will listen to the cry he utters here in his poem. For what was that sister, if not a lioness, a beacon of light, a prophet, comforting the others with her witness—including those who read the poem now, nearly a century and a half after the event—that we might be as startled by the Word as those on the *Deutschland* were, we too hovering in the liminal space of the imagination there in the "unshapeable shock night" of our own too-often chaotic world?

For isn't it true, as this young Jesuit had come to realize, that nothing happens by pure chance? Life is not some mere rolling of blind dice, as Nietzsche or Mallarmé or Thomas Hardy would have it. As it turned out, he sees now, the nuns perished sometime in the early hours of December 7, the eve of the Feast of the Immaculate Conception, "Feast of the one woman without stain," who, thus conceived, in turn so conceived her Son without stain. And now this nun, this virgin prophetess, in her turn conceives in her mind and heart the Word, "heart-throe, birth of a brain, "that héard and képt thee and úttered thee óutríght."

Out/right. Out and outwardly and rightly so, as Hopkins here writes it out on the page for us, inviting us to bear our witness as well. And the fruit of this cry, hers and his, is that her voice is heard, and will be heard again and again as her witness—read aright by the poet—makes clear, for she has indeed and *in deed* become a beacon in the dark: this bell—this belle—to "Startle the poor sheep back" and make of the shipwreck "a harvest" in the very heart of a tempest that tears away our chaff and leaves our sheer grain as gift for the Lord.

And something more: this is indeed Christ reenacting the harrowing of hell, "Our passion-plungèd giant risen" seeking out even "The-last-breath penitent spirits," so that he may return to the Father in the *De Processu*, the great procession out and back, Alpha and Omega, with his arms full of saved souls. This is, I think, the reason Hopkins could justify his poem: that others would see what he had gleaned from meditating on that winter storm and so turn back to the one reality that—as the Psalms tell us over and over again—contains everything that has ever finally mattered.

That Hopkins's great ode was rejected, not by the English public, but by his fellow Jesuits who edited the *Month*, because they found it too experimental, too cryptic, and certainly far too unsettling, only adds to the irony of one crying in the wilderness, though even that rejection Hopkins learned to live with. After all, if the poem was meant to be published and heeded, he believed, a way would be found, though it would take another four decades—thirty of them following his death—before the poem was finally published, and then by an old Oxford friend who was now England's Poet Laureate, Robert Bridges, the unlikely salvager who had little good to say about Catholics and even less about Jesuits. The important thing, of course, was that Hopkins remained true to the order that had done so much to shape the fire at the core of one of their own, and whose witness continues to bear the impress of the immortal diamond that the poem after all is.

It is also true that Hopkins's Jesuit witness became clearer as the years unfolded. Consider, for instance, the sonnets of 1877, written in the months leading up to his ordination in September of that year. Here, for instance, is the opening of a poem he wrote in February, called "God's Grandeur." "The world," the Jesuit poet reminds us, is indeed "chárged with the grandeur of God." There's a cosmic energy about God's Creation, Hopkins cries out, an electrical charge, both violent and yet violet sweet, which is ready to instress itself upon us if only we will pay it a moment of the attention it deserves. That grandeur which is God, Hopkins reminds us,

> will flame out, like shining from shook foil;
> It gathers to a greatness, like the ooze of oil
> Crushed. Why do men then now not reck his rod?
> Generations have trod, have trod, have trod;
>   And all is seared with trade; bleared, smeared with toil;
>   And wears man's smudge and shares man's smell: the soil
> Is bare now, nor can foot feel, being shod.
>
> And for all this, nature is never spent;
>   There lives the dearest freshness deep down things;
> And though the last lights off the black West went
>   Oh, morning, at the brown brink eastward, springs —
> Because the Holy Ghost over the bent
>   World broods with warm breast and with ah! bright wings. [15]

Note a couple of things here. First, the manner in which Hopkins addresses us, as if he were delivering a powerful homily in fourteen lines: that God's grandeur—*ad maiorem Dei gloriam*—is everywhere around us, not passively, but as a veritable force field, an energy. It is electrical, alive, ever-present, like a living river of crisp, fresh air. It is an energy that can strike us with its brilliance and force, the way a flash of lightning does, or the way light will instantly flare off gold or metal foil on a bright day, the way an insight strikes us all at once—as in a transformative instant whose memory remains vividly in the mind for decades to come,

Or it can touch us by increments, gathering to a greatness, a ripeness, the way luscious yellow-green olive oil collects in an olive press, drop by resplendent drop (as, say, in that oil press at Gethsemane, among the olive trees). So, Hopkins implies, grace struck Paul in an instant on his journey to Damascus and changed him forever.

Or it can come ever so slowly, like the tide, as it did for Augustine, after years of mistrials and willful mistakes. "Make me chaste, Oh Lord . . . but not yet!" But in either instance, it is Christ who is there in all of this, boding but abiding, whether it be the mental and spiritual suffering in the Garden of Olives, or the Eastering of the Son following the darkness of three dark days in the tomb.

Yes, Hopkins, that eco-poet, knew how generation after generation had trod, had trod, had trod, searing all of nature with its human smudge and smell and carbon footprint because we keep insisting on insulating ourselves from the living world around us with our own self-bent concerns and virtual nonrealities. No wonder he loved to walk barefoot whenever he could through the dew-fresh grass and feel the earth alive under his feet as he journeyed on.

Consider another sonnet written a week later, meditating this time on the night sky: "The Starlight Night" with its Van Gogh–like glinting heavens. "Look at the stars!," the poet invites us. Just look up at the incandescent heavens and

> all the fire-folk sitting in the air!
>   The bright boroughs, the circle-citadels there!
> Down in dim woods the diamond delves! the elves'-eyes!
> The grey lawns cold where gold, where quickgold lies!
>   Wind-beat whitebeam! airy abeles set on a flare!
> Flake-doves sent floating forth at a farmyard scare![16]

How beautiful, how wondrous is God's Creation, and there for the asking, the bidding. But bid with what, then? If you would see the Mystery that is there, the deepest mystery of it all, you will have to open yourself to what is being offered you, Hopkins tells us. But first you will have to rinse your eyes, rub them, yes, prepare them with "Prayer, patience, alms, vows." And behold, there before you: March bloom and May mess in every season, summer and winter. And yet, Hopkins tells us, all of this beauty is in the long run but a barn that merely holds the true beauty and the harvest, the shocks, the wheat, the surprise for which there are no adequate words. All of this natural beauty is but a paling, a fence, a pale reflection of something greater. And the stars, like tiny gold pieces, the outer gates containing a Mystery much greater, by which even our stupendous universe pales: the face of God, the Creator, our one true home, containing "Christ and his mother and all his hallows."

Of course Hopkins, like Cormac McCarthy in our time, would also become increasingly aware of the darker realities of life, of what he understood as the crushing effects of our fallen nature on the world itself. Once, after walking along the beaches of the Welsh working-class beach town of Rhyl, he compared the contrapuntal sound of the ocean waves and the "wild winch whirl" of the skylark's song to the sad carnival music men were too eager to make at a true cost hidden even from themselves. We—he wept—we who were "life's pride and cared-for crown," God's dear ones, darlings, had managed with our self-bent proclivities to lose "that cheer and charm of earth's past prime," as we rushed onward on our self-bent downward slope, breaking ourselves, down and "down / To man's last dust," radically destroying the possibilities we were heir to as we hurried unwittingly to the primal, Darwinian-laced sea from which we had evolved over millennia, draining backwards fast, ah, too fast—"towards man's first slime."[17]

Through all of Hopkins's suffering and pain—and he did suffer the loss of many connections to his family because of his conversion to the Roman Catholic Church, since they could not understand why their son and brother who had shown so much promise and had given up so much to become a Catholic and (worse) a Jesuit—in time he came to experience that "[t]o seem the stranger lies my lot, my life / Among strangers" as he confessed in a sonnet meant for no one's ears but his own. And one can feel that distancing in the photographs we have of his parents, his seven surviving brothers and sisters, his aunts and uncles and cousins—all at least nominally Church of England—and then compare these images with those of Hopkins the Jesuit. Then, too, there's a small book titled *Plain Reasons Against Joining the Church of Rome*, by Richard Frederick Littledale, LL.D., D.C.L., published in London by the Society for Promoting Christian Knowledge in 1880, a treatise written for "those who have seceded, or are tempted to secession, from the Church of England to the Roman Communion: that they may see what is the *true* nature of the accountability with which they are charging themselves in following their own private judgment rather than the providential order of God."[18]

There's a copy of the book in the Burns Library at Boston College inscribed by Hopkins's mother, Kate, dated April 2, 1881, and it suggests that she was still trying to understand why her poor boy had made the terrible decision he had fifteen years earlier to leave the Anglican fold while a student at Oxford. "Father and mother dear, / Brothers and sisters are in Christ not near," Hopkins would write in May 1885 in a poem he never shared with anyone, much less his own family. He wrote that poem a year into his assignment as a professor and university examiner in classics in his time in Ireland, exiled at forty to the Jesuits' University College in crumbling Dublin. If coming into the Church had been something he felt he had had to do if he was to find peace within himself, that peace had also turned out to be—as his Master had warned—a parting as well, his own "sword and strife."[19]

Then too there was his work as a priest ministering to the largely working-class Irish populace in a huge industrial city like Liverpool in the late 1870s and early '80s. Assigned to the large neo-baroque Jesuit parish of St. Francis Xavier on Salisbury Street, he assumed pastoral duties including, among other responsibilities, saying Mass, preparing sermons, hearing confessions with the smell of whiskey on many of his penitents, visiting the sick, counseling, and performing the last rites. He did not have the rhetorical eloquence of some of his fellow Jesuits, as he himself confessed, and phrases like "The Loss of God's First Kingdom" in one sermon and the word "Sweetheart" in another soon got him in trouble with his Jesuit superior, who suggested that Fr. Hopkins write out his sermons beforehand so that he could look over them before Hopkins delivered them.

On the fourth Sunday after Easter, April 25, 1880, he told his congregation of Irish draymen and dockworkers that they should heed what he had to say about John's Gospel and Christ's long last testament and not "stare or sleep over" what he was going to tell them, because it was, after all, both "contemptible and unmanly . . . for men whose minds are naturally clear, to give up at the first hearing of a hard passage in the Scripture" and "to care to know no more than children know" about the Word of God. On this particular day he asked them to take to heart a passage in which Jesus tells his disciples that, though he would soon leave them, the Holy Ghost would come in his place. *"And when he, that is the Holy Ghost,"* he told them from the raised lectern, *"whom our Lord in this place calls the Paraclete, has come he will convince the world of sin and of justice and of judgment."*[20]

Now it would be his task to explain to his congregation—and he could already see one or two beginning to nod off as one of the ushers prodded them awake with a cane—what exactly a Paraclete is. A Paraclete, he told them, is someone "who comforts, who cheers, who encourages, who persuades, who exhorts, who stirs up, who urges forward, who calls [us] on." And then he brought the idea home with an example from one of those cricket matches they had all no doubt attended. "You have seen at cricket how when one of the batsmen at the wicket has made a hit and wants to score a run, the other doubts, hangs back, or is ready to run in again, how eagerly the first will cry, *"Come on, come on."* Well, he explained in his down-to-earth fashion, that is what a Paraclete does to someone, "calling him on, springing to meet him half way, crying to his ears or to his heart: This way to do God's will, this way to save your soul, come on, come on!"

And now he had warmed to it. Christ, too, he told his congregation, was himself a Paraclete, for didn't he urge on his disciples with his own example? Didn't he lead the way himself, like an officer of the line before his troops as they headed into danger? And when, like Peter, his trusted disciples had fled when the temple police and Roman soldiers ambushed them in the garden at Gethsemane, when the lanterns cast long shadows among the olive trees, didn't he bear "the brunt of battle alone," dying alone there on the field on Calvary hill and bring "the victory by his blood"?

Didn't he cry his men on, telling them to follow him, until, finally, they did just that? And when, sadly, "they would not follow, he let them go and took all the war upon himself. . . . For though Christ cheered them on they feared to follow, though the Captain led the way the soldiers fell back; he was not for that time a successful Paraclete," for, when the moment of truth finally came to be counted, didn't they to a man "forsake him and flee"?

How hard to do good in this world, this young priest knew. For our very "flesh is against it, the world is against it, the Devil is against it." And yet, didn't Christ prevail? For with his final victory over the darkness "the hellish head was crushed," though "the earthly members were not aware of a wound." Yes, he went on that Sunday morning, how he wished he could hold their attention a while longer and show them "how the Holy Ghost has followed and will follow up this first beginning, convincing and converting nation after nation and age after age till the whole earth is hereafter to be covered." Oh, how he would like to show them just a few of the ways by which "the thousand thousand tongues" of the Holy Spirit worked their wonders, back then in Jerusalem, as now, here, in Liverpool.[21]

But there was no more time.

No time. No time. During that same Mass, he read off the names of those in the parish who had recently died. Among them was one Felix Spencer, a blacksmith who had lived on Birchfield Street and who had died of pulmonary tuberculosis four days earlier at the age of thirty-one. Soon after, Hopkins composed one of the few poems he wrote during his time at Liverpool, a sonnet called "Felix Randal," the word "randal" being derived from the Old English and meaning a shield, a strip of leather placed between a horse's hoof and the horseshoe, as a way of protecting the horse's foot. It's the perfect word for what Hopkins wants here: the sense of the holy viaticum he had offered the dying farrier to help him on his final journey beyond death. "Felix Randal the farrier, O is he dead then?" the poet-priest begins, as if surprised to learn that Felix should be so soon gone. And is the priest's "duty all ended" now? Or is there one last thing he must do to honor poor Felix? And did he not watch this "mould of man," no matter his human strength as it returned—as it had to—to the mold of clay from whence it came, dust to dust, this man,

> big-boned and hardy-handsome
> Pining, pining, till time when reason rambled in it, and some
> Fatal four disorders, fleshed there, all contended? [22]

So it is with death, no matter how many of the dying—young and old—he has had to watch over and must in the future watch over, offering them the dignity of the last rites: the anointing, the confession, and the offering of Christ's own body as a shield against the Dark One's final onslaught. "Sickness broke him," the poet tells us, remembering how this young blacksmith had cursed his fate at first, unwilling to believe that someone as strong as himself could succumb to a wasting disease that would take him, as death takes us all. But the priest had also seen Felix changing under his ministering, how anointing him with the oil of the sick had comforted him, and how he had then offered Felix the "sweet reprieve" of confession, and tendered him the "ransom" of Holy Communion: Christ's gift of himself as payment for Felix's human failings, the price Christ had offered up most tenderly. *Forgive them, Father.* . . .

And then the traditional Lancashire blessing and farewell: "Ah well, God rest him all road ever he offended!" Life as a journey, then: that age-old metaphor—a plodding on of our quotidian lives, like workhorses in the grinding going round of work. And yet, and yet: that surprising, transfiguring ending of the poem, as Felix's "more boisterous years" give way inevitably to suffering and death, but then, in turn, the old self gives way to a radically new self, prefigured already in the old, as the poet recalls a time when *thou*, Felix, "at the random grim forge, powerful amidst peers / Didst fettle for the great grey drayhorse his bright & battering sandal!"

The reverence of that "thou," as Felix enters the Great Mystery of returning to his Father. Just so, then, that what Felix did for those great grey dray horses drumming the cobbled streets of Liverpool, Fr. Hopkins has been privileged to do for Felix. Thus, in its closing lines, the poem circles back to Felix's prime, at the same time crossing the threshold of a mystery outside of time as we know it, as blessed Felix—for that is what Felix's name means, the Latin of the first name soldered to the Old English of Randal—enters his new life armed with his bright

HOPKINS AND THE POETICS OF JESUIT SPIRITUALITY

and battering sandal, his sacramental armor, the humble image of the horseshoe signaling the Omega, our true end point, as Felix goes forth to meet his beloved Lord and Master.

Hopkins spent much of the six and a half years between his ordination and the time when he was missioned to Dublin to teach Latin and Greek to Irish Catholic university students (not unlike James Joyce) working as select preacher in places as diverse as London, Oxford, Stonyhurst, Glasgow, Manchester, and Liverpool. In that time, hard as it was for a man who confessed that he often suffered from melancholy, or what we call depression, at least he was in England. And then came the call to leave his homeland for Ireland, something he found particularly hard to do, as he saw it as nothing less than exile from his "rare, dear England." His dream had always been to work in England and do what he could to restore his beloved country to the faith of an earlier time, the faith of Bede and Langland and Chaucer and Duns Scotus and Thomas More—a time when England was still in communion with Rome.

Instead, at thirty-nine, he found himself in Ireland in a time when the country was in a state of profound national unrest and was increasingly demanding autonomy or at least parity with England, such as many believed Home Rule would provide. And here he was, the only English Jesuit in Dublin, teaching mostly poor Irish Catholic university students in what, in the time of Swift and Goldsmith, had been England's second capital, and where the Catholic majority had been largely excluded from Dublin's Trinity College, much as they had been from Oxford and Cambridge.

"I am in Ireland now," Hopkins wrote. "Now I am at a third / Remove," religion, family, and now country separating him from the world that had nurtured him. But, being Hopkins, he refused to pity himself. "Not but in *all* removes I can / Kind love both give and get." Still, there was this to ponder as well: that he was suffering depression and even separation, he believed, from the very one whose one "word / Wisest" had sustained him until now, and even his poems, scratched out in longhand on random sheets of paper, seemed barred from seeing the light of day as if by "dark heaven's baffling ban." Or if not heaven's strange ban, then—worse— "hell's spell." And it was this—to have no audience for his singular and original poems, no one, not his Jesuit brothers and not even his closest friend, Robert Bridges—that is the key to understanding what he had tried to do in his poems. This, then, was what it meant "to hoard unheard" or if heard then to go unheeded, which left him in essence "a lonely began."[23] Not a beginning, but a "began," which—over and over again seemed to go nowhere.

But it is "in the deepest darkness," the Trappist Father Thomas Merton tells us, "that we most fully possess God on earth, because it is then that our minds are most truly liberated from the weak, created lights that are darkness in comparison to Him." For only then are we "filled with his infinite Light which seems pure darkness to our reason." This is what Hopkins, like St. John of the Cross before him and St. Teresa of Calcutta after him, had to learn: that it was only in darkness that "the infinite God Himself becomes the Light of the darkened soul and possesses it entirely with His Truth." Then, and only then, "at this inexplicable moment," did the deepest night become day and faith itself turned into understanding.[24]

In the beginning was the Word, John's Gospel begins, and the Word was with God, and the Word was God: that promise, that bold promise. And against that, what? To be stillborn, to sing into an apparent Void the message Hopkins believed he had been sent to announce and that we—the fortunate ones—have been able to listen to and learn from the witness of what his friend Canon Richard Watson Dixon called Hopkins's "terrible sonnets," terrible in the biblical sense, as we glean such consolation as we can from another man's sorrow. But then, is this not one of the deep paradoxes of the Christian message itself?

There is so much that Hopkins has to offer us that it takes months, indeed years, to plumb what he has to teach us—in his sermons, letters, lecture notes, his intimate diaries, his meditations on the *Spiritual*

Exercises, but especially in his poems. And since there is only so much one can cover, let's focus on a few examples, such as "The Windhover," the poem Hopkins wrote in the months leading up to his ordination. He composed a full draft of the poem on May 30, 1877, while he was still at St. Beuno's, conceived, apparently, as he walked out with a group of fellow Jesuits to celebrate a May morning Mass in the small stone chapel situated out in the fields beyond the main house. That the Mass was a memorial for the French martyr Joan of Arc was no mere chance, not for the priest who had written so beautifully of those five Franciscan nuns, or of St. Thecla, or of Margaret Clitheroe, or on so many occasions remembering Mary, his spiritual mother.

"I caught this morning morning's minion," the poem begins, as the speaker's eye follows the pattern of a kestrel, a small hawk, hovering high in the morning sky above. But this is more than a bird. This is Christ's self the bird inscapes upon the poet alert to God's presence in all things. This bird is indeed nothing less than the "king / dom of daylight's dauphin," a "dapple-dawn-drawn Falcon," drawn toward the dappling sun, the eastering light, but also drawn—etched out—against that same light, a thing gliding effortlessly above him in the winds blowing in off the ocean.

What is it the poet, steeped in the Ignatian method of prayer with its focus on the sacramental mystery of God's Creation, a method that centers on the bread of the quotidian transformed into a veritable sacrament, what *is* it he sees? A bird, yes, ringing out its *quidditas*, its doing-be, its uniqueness, as it navigates without effort through the strong headland winds, perfectly attuned—this creature—to a world it and the poet both inhabit. Ah, the mystery and the mastery of the thing!

But Hopkins being Hopkins, he sees more, much more, as he watches the falcon swing through the air in wide circles, before finally plunging to earth to seize upon what it has been searching for. Isn't that what he understands Christ has done with us? Singled each of us out, descending on the observer here, now, on this cool spring wind-gusting morning, as once Christ singled out a young French maiden who would wring victory for her king, though at what terrible cost to herself? But then, of course, isn't that what Christ Himself experienced in his emptying of himself for humankind? Beautiful as he was as a man and a teacher and a friend, who bestowed his wisdom on any who had ears to listen, someone Hopkins confessed he would very much loved to have met in the flesh, what Christ did in giving himself up on the cross, his body buckling there on the wood, was something "a billion times told lovelier, more dangerous," Hopkins confesses here, now, in his poem.

But, the poet asks, is that really so unlike the way things work in nature, where clods of earth and pieces of coal should buckle, crumple, break up in order to realize another, far more striking beauty hidden within themselves? Look at the Welsh farmers with their horses in the countryside about him, breaking up the moist clods of earth: how the light shines upon them, catching the quartz glints, in an instant turning them into diamondlike shards of light—"sheer plod" itself doing this, allowing the plow and the sillion both to shine in God's light.

Or—evoking the words of another priest, this one his beloved George Herbert as he sighs with his own "ah my dear" addressed to Christ—isn't that what happens when those seemingly dead coals there in the grating of his room, as in the gratings of millions of hearths, those "blue-bleak embers" that, even as they fall, "gall themselves, and gash gold-vermillion," flaming out even as they die—like Christ on the cross, giving everything of himself for us, and in the process transforming the world itself? There it is, then, the thing that saves us in the daily going round of things: unstinting service to others in that endless supply of papers to grade and students to see through the straits of Homer and Plato and Cicero and Seneca, or Sappho and Catullus, or Ovid and Livy and Pliny, all the while having to deal with sickness and fever and depression, while trying to buck oneself up by keeping one's sense of wit and humor about one.

Hopkins was forty-four when he succumbed to typhoid there at 85-86 St. Stephen's Green, Dublin, only to be buried, not back in England, but somewhere in the Jesuits' community plot, without a headstone, just like his fellow Jesuits, in Dublin's Glasnevin Cemetery. For over half a century now he has served as a model for me, both as a poet and as a man who served God as he could. Not a day goes by that I don't think of him, so much so that I often feel his presence about me.

Here's a poem of mine dedicated to the Jesuits I have been honored to know and work with over the years, including my own Jesuit son. I wrote it to accompany an iconic image by Fr. William Hart McNichols, which was published in *America* in January, 2005. "Hopkins in Ireland" is a Petrarchan sonnet, in honor of Hopkins's own signature form:

Above the blue-bleak priest the bright-blue fisher hovers.
The priest notes the book upon the table, the lamp beside the book.
A towering Babel of papers still to grade, and that faraway look
as once more the mind begins to wander. Ah, to creep beneath the covers

of the belled bed beckoning across the room. He stops, recovers,
takes another sip of bitter tea, then winces as he takes another look
at the questions he has posed his students and the twists they took
to cover up their benighted sense of Latin. The fisher hovers

like a lit match closer to him. The windows have all been shut against
the damp black Dublin night. After all these years, his collar chokes
him still, in spite of which he wears it like some outmoded mark
of honor, remembering how his dear Ignatius must have sensed
the same landlocked frustrations. Again he lifts his pen. His strokes
lash out against the dragon din of error. The fisher incandesces in the dark. [25]

The Kingfisher, Fisher of Men: the dark dove who hovers above us because God knows what we ourselves too often forget, that, as Hopkins wrote in the months leading up to his death, if he often felt like some grunt, some soldier tossed about from assignment to assignment, some "Jack, joke, poor potsherd, patch, matchwood," he was also—like us, as he affirmed with one of the strongest uses of the verb *Is* I know of in the language (the verb and Verbum of being and becoming)—"immortal diamond," not because of anything we had done, but because of God's mercy and love in becoming one of us.

In the last year of his life, despite his crippling bouts of illness and depression, he seems to have found a sense of consolation that went deeper than what he had experienced earlier, no doubt because he had walked through the valley of the shadow of death himself and understood more deeply what was at stake here: what in fact would have to be left, not in his hands, but in God's. Here is the poem, a caudated (or extended) sonnet, a sonnet with tails, because it would have to burst the boundaries of the traditional sonnet to get said what had to be said. He called the poem "That Nature is a Heraclitean Fire and of the comfort of the Resurrection," and he composed it in late July 1888, as he walked about the streets of Dublin, trying to clear his head and rest his tired eyes after one more day of grading examinations.

In Ireland, they say, it rains between the showers. And so here, as this time a summer storm rather than the winter storm he had written about in his *Deutschland* ode a dozen years before races across Ireland and England from west to east. Rain, snow, rain, snow, winter, spring, summer, fall: the same and yet different, again and again and again in the great Heraclitean flux of nature.

As beautiful and vital and frisky as the clouds appear to be this Saturday afternoon in late July in the city, as the rains pass by and the summer sun begins to break through again, it strikes him with the force of a revelation that these clouds are more than mere clouds: that they are in fact a fast forwarding of life itself, and that for all of their casual roughness, like a gang of rowdies passing overhead, they—like time itself—are careless of the changes they make on everything. They are, in fact, the vast smoke from some great bonfire.

Bonfire: not a bonny fire but rather what the word really derives from: *bone fire*—and one that will consume us all in the great conflagration of time, including the poet who witnesses the scene of apocalyptic light flaring across the whitewashed cottages and buildings with a growing terror. "Cloud-puffball," the poem begins with a kind of hullabaloo, as if he were witnessing an Irish St. Patty's Day parade, or a political demonstration in the streets:

> torn tufts, tossed pillows | flaunt forth, then chevy on an air-
> Built thoroughfare: heaven-roysterers, in gay-gangs | they throng; they
> glitter in marches.
> Down roughcast, down dazzling whitewash, | wherever an elm arches,
> Shivelights and shadowtackle ín long | lashes lace, lance, and pair.
> Delightfully the bright wind boisterous | ropes, wrestles, beats earth bare
> Of yestertempest's creases; | in pool and rut peel parches
> Squandering ooze to squeezed | dough, crust, dust; stanches, starches
> Squadroned masks and manmarks | treadmire toil there
> Footfretted in it. Million-fuelèd, | nature's bonfire burns on.[26]

Pools to mud to squeezed dough to crust to dust, until in short order the wheel tracks of wagons and carriages and the etched boot- and footprints in the street disappear, as every soul on the streets of Dublin that afternoon long ago disappeared. And as he will soon disappear, as Merton said to his Bangkok audience just hours before he died when he touched a fan with faulty wiring and the electric shock killed him.

And then we are gone, and—in short order—the memory of who we were going up in the bonfire, along with our life's work, our stories, our poems, our papyrus leavings, yes, even the things we leave in our virtual clouds today. "Quench her bonniest, dearest | to her, her clearest-selvèd spark / Man," this Jesuit, versed in the *Exercises* too well knows, then

> how fast his firedint, | his mark on mind, is gone!
> Both are in an unfathomable, all is in an enormous dark
> Drowned. O pity and indig | nation! Manshape, that shone
> Sheer off, disseveral, a star, | death blots black out; nor mark
> Is any of him at all so stark
> But vastness blurs and time | beats level.

And then? What then? Right there, in the split second marked by the pause in the middle of a line of poetry, the clarion call of Eternity breaks through and into our sense of chthonic time, time as evolution, and there comes the sudden transformation, as St. Paul explained to the community at Thessalonica, and the chord of a new dimension, a new reality, is sounded. "Enough," the poet exclaims, and there it is, what the heart has always hungered for: "the Resurrection, / A heart's-clarion!" And so, from desolation to consolation, in a flash, full:

> Away grief's gasping, | joyless days, dejection.
> Across my foundering deck shone
> A beacon, an eternal beam.

We are sinking, Lord, the poet remembers, recalling, too, Jesus in that fishing boat being awakened by his terrified followers, pleading with him that now they were sinking, that the boat was in danger of going under. And Jesus, rising up to face the hellish waves, and quieting them with his words. Like that tall German nun on the *Deutschland*, calling out to the only one who could save her now, save what was essential: her very self. And now it is Fr. Hopkins himself, calling out to the only One who can save him from time's vast womb of all, home of all night. And so, with Christ at his side he can afford to be jaunty once more. Let death take it all, he says. Let "Flesh fade, and mortal trash / Fall to the residuary worm" as one's will and last testament are read out. Yes, go on, let the "world's wildfire leave but ash." No matter now, no matter. Because, in an instant, "In a flash, at a trumpet crash," as Paul had realized a mere two millennia before, the faithful would be at rest with Christ.

And why? Because, as John Duns Scotus had underlined centuries earlier at Oxford, the Lord of the Universe had deigned to become one of us, had emptied Himself of his Godhead to walk among us for love. Because the great *"I AM"* had mingled His Being with ours, thus raising us to the level of the Godhead, making us His children. "I am all at once what Christ is, I since he was what I am," Hopkins wrote, instressing the fact in and upon us in a series of fourteen monosyllables back to back, because

> I am all at once what Christ is, I since he was what I am, and
> This Jack, joke, poor potsherd, I patch, matchwood, immortal diamond,
> Is immortal diamond.

Something immortal exists at the core of our being, and it will shine forth when all the nonessentials are burned away, and the times when we were merely one more Jack or Joe or Tom or Molly, the times when we were dismissed or dismissed ourselves as some joke, the times when we were but a mere fragment—a poor potsherd—of who we might have been—a patch, a clown (*pagliaccio*), a near nonentity, a piece of matchwood to be struck, to flare up, and be extinguished, and yet, having undergone the ordeal, having carried the wood of the cross, would match as best he could his wood with the wood of Christ's cross, we too—because of God's mercy—are, when all is said and done, "immortal diamond."

Diamond, which Hopkins rhymes with "I am, and" reinforcing that with the final dental *t* of what—*"tiamand"* and *diamond*: a word in the center of which shines, *"I am."* Not merely I was once upon a time, the dates engraved on our tombstone, but *I AM*: the name by which God identified himself to Moses, a phrase that John the Evangelist echoes again and again as the living signature of the Son, and that the Father, in his infinite goodness, has given us to share. Let the poems, then, like the example of this poet-priest's life, in spite of its often blue-bleak soutane exterior, bear witness to the truth of his life (and ours) that is at one and the same time, and amid the Heraclitean flux of our contingent existences—a resounding and final affirmation, as Hopkins has come in time to understand—of God's abiding love.

Then it was back to ordinary time, as the journey continued and Hopkins understood, good Jesuit that he was, that it was in remaining faithful to the duties assigned him, even here in Dublin, perhaps especially here in Dublin, that he might paradoxically grow in his union with the Triune God.

Three months later, in October, at the request of his fellow Jesuit Fr. Goldie, Hopkins wrote a sonnet in honor of a Jesuit brother whose first feast day occurred that same month. This was Alphonsus Rodriguez, born some 350 years earlier, a "simple" Jesuit brother whose main task had been to welcome guests at the gate of the Jesuit house of studies in Majorca. And though he had wanted to be a Jesuit priest, the death of his father in Segovia had left him with the responsibility of taking over the family's business selling cloth. In time he had married a woman named Maria, and soon he was the father of three. And then Maria and all three children died, and in time even the cloth business failed.

Adrift, he eventually joined the Jesuits, hoping to become a priest, only to be told that at thirty-five he was too old to begin the long course of studies leading to ordination and so would have to settle on being a brother. Two years later, he was sent to Majorca, where he was assigned the duty of porter. A humble task, yes, but he took it seriously, much as Hopkins tried to fulfill the duties assigned him, Alphonsus saying to himself, as he went to answer the door each time, "I'm coming, Lord." Fast-forward another thirty-five years, and there was Brother Alphonsus, still answering the door, still calling on Christ. It was then that he met Peter Claver, a Jesuit in formation, and became Claver's spiritual director.

It was Alphonsus who, with his keen spiritual insights into the interior life of Claver as with so many others, urged the young Jesuit to offer himself to the missions in South America. In time Claver was sent to Cartagena, Colombia, to work with thousands of West African slaves who were being forcibly shipped to the New World. Claver it was who fed and tended and comforted many of these enslaved human beings over the years, bearing witness to their dignity and humanity, so that in time he would earn the title "Slave of the Slaves." And only now, in 1888, Alphonsus would be canonized not for his brilliant exploits, but for a life of humility served in the name of Christ. He was, really, exactly the sort of saint Hopkins could relate to, and the poem Hopkins wrote in Alphonsus's honor tells us as much about Hopkins's own kind of heroism as it tells us about the saint he set out to honor.

"Honour is flashed off exploit," Hopkins begins, and then adds the all-important qualifier: "or so we say." And, yes, it is fitting that

> those strokes once that gashed flesh or galled shield
> Should tongue that time now, trumpet now that field,
> And, on the fighter, forge his glorious day.[27]

For so it was with Christ, who underwent the long journeys from town to town proclaiming the Word, then the betrayal and the savage torture at the pillar, the crowning with thorns, the being forced through the streets of the ancient city, only to be nailed hands and feet to a cross, like some hawk to a barn door. Thus, too, with so many martyrs, from St. Stephen on, who have borne witness to Christ.

But what if the war should be fought *within*, as with those who suffer depression and self-loathing or what we call post-traumatic stress disorder—the awful sense that everything one has done has ended up a failure? What then? What then, when "Earth hears no hurtle from fiercest fray"? What if one is missioned to teach students, many of whom couldn't care less about Latin and Greek or English? And what of those long hours of grading paper after paper after paper, of trying to right grammatical wrongs that only seem to proliferate like cancer?

This is God's work, finally, to judge, not ours, for it is His to crown his suffering servant and wring victory out of the jaws of sullen defeat:

> Yet God (that hews mountain and continent,
> Earth, all, out; who, with trickling increment,
> Veins violets and tall trees makes more and more)
> Could crowd career with conquest while there went
> Those years and years by of world without event
> That in Majorca Alfonso watched the door.

It was a powerful lesson that Hopkins could only learn, finally, by suffering through a similar world that seemed to pass him by as well without event, even as the Holy Spirit consoled him with the gift of composing poems of suffering and marginalization that speak as powerfully to us today as when Hopkins first penned them in his cell-like room on St. Stephen's Green.

By the spring of 1889 it was clear that something was seriously wrong with Hopkins's health. He was physically and mentally exhausted, and there was an ironic edge to his letters to Bridges, especially about Bridges's insistence on publishing his own poetry only in limited editions, rather than reaching out to a wider audience available in inexpensive paperbacks. Bridges did not take kindly to Hopkins's good-natured joking, and he wrote back to remind Hopkins that at least *he* was being published, while his friend remained unpublished and, yes, unknown to nearly everyone beside himself. He even went so far as to burn two of Hopkins's final letters to him, an act that Bridges soon enough regretted.

For his part, realizing that he had managed to offend Bridges when what he had hoped to do was to urge his friend to seek out a wider readership, Hopkins apologized. "I am ill to-day," he wrote Bridges on April 29, 1989, "but, no matter for that as my spirits are good." Then he added, "I want you to 'buck-up,' as we used to say at school, about those jokes over which you write in so dudgeonous a spirit. . . . You I treated to the same sort of irony as I do myself; but it is true it makes all the world of difference whose hand administers."[28] As a peace offering and apologia, he enclosed a new sonnet, this one addressed to Bridges himself, which he had written the previous week.

It would be his final poem, and in it he tried to explain to Bridges why he wrote so little these days, and why he let the things he did write "lie months and years in rough copy untransferred" to the book of poems Bridges had copied out for him years before. He began the poem with an announcement of sorts, describing the "fine delight" that came with poetic inspiration. It was a sensual image, really, for inspiration was rather like a phallic fire, not unlike the moment of spiritual impregnation such as Mary experienced at the Annunciation, when she gave her consent to the angel that she would do what had been asked of her, regardless of the consequences:

> The fine delight that fathers thought; the strong
> Spur, live and lancing like the blowpipe flame,
> Breathes once and, quenchèd faster than it came,
> Leaves yet the mind a mother of immortal song.[29]

That moment of conception, of poetic inspiration, Hopkins went on, was all that was necessary to generate a poem, even if it took months, even years, as the poet Horace had said, for the poem to come to fruition. Still, the seed had been planted, and the poem would come in its own good time:

> Nine months she then, nay years, nine years she long
> Within her wears, bears, cares and moulds the same:
> The widow of an insight lost she lives, with aim
> Now known and hand at work now never wrong.

That moment of inspiration, he confessed now, was what he needed if his own muse was to be impregnated: the ecstatic and sensuous rapture of insight, the sense that the gist of the poem had been conceived, the sense too of the Holy Spirit, the Paraclete, speaking as in tongues of fire, that "Sweet fire the sire of muse," and the "one rapture of an inspiration."

But, he explained, that was what was missing now. In the rhythm of the lines that followed, he gave Bridges the very thing he said he did not have. "O then," he wrote, "if in my lagging lines you miss / The roll, the rise, the carol, the creation," blame it on the desolation of "the winter world" he now found himself blanketed by, a world where he could scarcely breathe "that bliss / Now," so that he had to offer up "with some sighs, our explanation."

And therein lay the answer, for it was not "my explanation," he wrote, but rather "our explanation." And who was this "our"? Was it himself speaking to himself in his winter world, or was it rather himself and what Wallace Stevens called his "interior paramour," his understanding that just here was where his Lord and Master had placed him now, so that even in the midst of desolation, in the midst of what the artist might feel as a prolonged dry spell, he could still create an extraordinary poem that reflected and incarnated the very fire, the very roll and rise and carol of creation, that he said he now lacked. Even in his desolation, then, Hopkins found consolation, and if his friend did not understand, well, at least Hopkins and the Holy Spirit that sustained him now—his own interior paramour—understood.

If he was a physical wreck by then, suffering from migraines, eyestrain, eczema, stomach reflux, insomnia, and—worse—typhoid contacted by flea-infested rats in the sewer of the school's kitchen, which he thought at first was just some rheumatic fever that had left him prostrate, no matter. "I saw a doctor yesterday," he wrote his father on May 3, in the joking spirit they had employed with each other over the years, "who treated my complaint as a fleabite, a treatment which begets confidence but not gratitude."

For a month, though bedridden and tended by nurses, he seemed to rally. But then, during the night of June 5, his condition took a turn for the worse, and his parents back in England were told that their son's end was near. They were both there at his side when he died on Saturday, June 8, at half past one in the afternoon.

His last words are reported to have been, "I am so happy. I am so happy." His funeral took place three days later at the Church of St. Francis Xavier's on Upper Gardiner Street in Dublin, with seventy priests and a huge crowd in attendance, after which his body was laid to rest in an unmarked grave in Glasnevin Cemetery, in the Jesuits' crowded plot, his name incised, along with the names of his fellow Jesuits, on the granite headstone you will find there today.

2
THE HAVOC AND
THE GLORY

A confession. No one—not Williams or Hart Crane or Berryman or Lowell or even Wallace Stevens—has touched me as deeply as Hopkins has. There are other poets and writers whose lives I would love to have written if I had another twenty or thirty years, which I know I do not. There's T. S. Eliot and Yeats, Joyce and Frost and Auden, Elizabeth Bishop and Flannery O'Connor, to name but a few. Then, too, there's my fascination with John Donne and George Herbert and Keats. But always I seem to return to Hopkins as my deepest inspiration, the figure who has continued to speak most deeply to me over the past half century and more, even when I was engrossed in the lives of other poets.

The books, articles, lectures, letters, photocopies, e-mails, and manuscripts have piled up now longer than the forty-four years Hopkins was with us. The—what shall I call it—obsession began for me in the spring of '62, when I read "The Wreck of the Deutschland" for a senior English class at Manhattan College—an attic room with its slant gelid light, the faces of my classmates, all men in those days, bored, overworked, sleep-deprived, hungover. Still, in poring over that ode for the first time, something hit, something like lightning, though it was at the same time as gentle and consoling as oil or balm. And the instress of it: that sense of another's abrupt self entering me through the self's sakes and keepings has stayed with me ever since.

Fast-forward another half dozen years, to Hunter College, when I began writing my commentary on the sonnets of Hopkins, married now and the father of three sons, teaching freshmen by day and secretaries by night, as well as classes in the humanities at the John Jay College of Criminal Justice, which was then housed at the Police Academy on East 23rd, teaching New York's finest, Frank Serpico among them. The sheer manic chutzpah of it all: to have undertaken to write a commentary on Hopkins at twenty-six. But there it was: a way for one brand-new PhD to break into the world of academe in rural western Massachusetts, replete with its brinded cows and the odd poplar or two among the heavy maples.

Then other voices calling, the dead rising against the windows of the twenty-six-story library there in Amherst, their outlines fluttering against the gray panes, demanding to be blooded: William Carlos Williams and his Jersey landscapes first (a dozen years), then John Berryman, who rudely shoved Robert Lowell aside and demanded that I attend to him first and then return to Cal. After all, if Virgil could gently muscle Dante aside, as he had with Allen Mandelbaum—my own mentor—so that the *Aeneid* took precedence over the completion of the *Divine Comedy* for several years at least, then surely Berryman—as Berryman himself once told me in a dream—might take priority over Lowell, his delicious *Dream Songs* demanding at least *that* much acknowledgment.

Fast-forward another twelve years, and both ghosts fed with my life's blood in the shape of two more biographies. Then the noble, self-destructive figure of Hart Crane advancing toward me, the one who had waited in the wings, tap-dancing there for a quarter of a century, winking and saying—*pace* Augustine—"Wasn't it me you were looking for?" And so another five years before his life could be told.

The trouble—the havoc and the glory of the whole biographical enterprise—is that the would-be biographer sees that, unlike so many others who have claimed the name *poet*, Hopkins has grown immensely with the years as well. And so now I look back over half a century of teaching British and Irish and American poetry, and watch as the literary canon has shifted and changed. Many poets who were important to me at thirty or forty or even fifty fall away or reconfigure themselves, while a few like Hopkins continue to grow in majesty and stature.

Is he a major minor poet, or a minor major one? Or is he—as Philip Levine wrote me ten years ago—the premier poet of the past 150 years? And is it poetry we should use to measure the man? What about Hopkins as thinker? Or, what the young Robert Lowell considered even more important, what about Hopkins as *saint*?

How *does* one finally measure Hopkins? Was he really an eccentric? Eccentric: surely it is a word that crops up everywhere, among Hopkins's Jesuit superiors and colleagues, certainly, but also among those Victorian writers who came in contact with him and were puzzled by what they saw and heard: Lang, Gosse, Caine, Rossetti, Kate Tynan, and Yeats. Even Robert Bridges.

How does one come to read the man adequately? So much important work has been done in the past half century, and by so many—the late Norman MacKenzie and his daughter Catherine Phillips clearly among them—and so much is still being done. There is the work of placing Hopkins within his own Jesuit milieu, scholarship being done by at least three Jesuits: Frs. Schlatter, Barber, and Feeney. Work, too, on Hopkins as Latin and Greek scholar, work on his music, work on his understanding of the *Spiritual Exercises*, work on the nature of his mission talks and sermons, delivered to mostly working-class Irish and Scots-Irish Catholics as well as old English Catholic families. And the truth is we need all of these windows in order to see more clearly the various ways in which Hopkins can be better understood.

The venture has turned out to be more complex than many have allowed, in part because the Jesuit response to Hopkins himself was so varied and complex, riding the spectrum from those like Frs. Joseph Rickaby and Francis Bacon who understood something of his genius, or those superiors like Frs. Galway and Jones who were kind to him, to those like his no-nonsense superior, Fr. Purbrick, who found Hopkins— how shall we say this—expendable enough to be the only English Jesuit he could spare for the new Irish Catholic university being set up where John Henry Newman's noble dream had foundered years before.[30]

There is, too, the Anglo-Irish connection to refurbish, at once more complex and more cosmopolitan than we had previously guessed, with figures like the renegade Fr. Martial Klein, SJ, and the Anglo-Irish Judge O'Hagan. Or the poet Kate Tynan and the young, brilliant epileptic Jesuit mathematician Brother Robert Curtis, and Jack Yeats and Jack's son, William Butler Yeats, adding to the mix. Then too there's the playful and hopeful Hopkins to consider, over against his exhausted and despondent Doppelgänger.

An example: when, in the fall of 1882 Bridges sent Hopkins the manuscript of his drama *Prometheus the Firegiver*, Hopkins wrote back that, while he found much to like about the play, he also thought the opening lines were the worst in the entire play, and—coming just there—he hoped Bridges might rework them. These are the lines:

> From high Olympus and the domeless courts,
> Where mighty Zeus our angry king confirms
> The Fates' decrees and bends the will of the gods,
> I come: and on the earth step with glad foot.

For starters, he explained, "domeless" would have to go. It made no sense. Bridges wrote back: What was wrong with *domeless*, a word he particularly favored? Given the historic time frame, it was "not archaeologically right," Hopkins explained, "though I believe the so-called Tomb or Treasury of Atreus has a rude dome." Nor did it "convey much image," to Hopkins's mind. But Bridges insisted. What exactly was wrong here? Did Hopkins want him to replace the whole four lines?! "I have told you of my objection to *domeless*," Hopkins wrote back, warming to it now. "If there were some reason for it why do you not tell me? A court I suppose to be any large room or space of a building upon the ground floor and imperfectly closed. . . . Courts can seldom be domed in any case, so that it is needless to tell us that those on Olympus are domeless."

With this, he was off on a tear. No: better to say the kamptulicon-less courts, *Kamptulicon* being the brand name for a floor cloth made up of cork and India rubber. Surely the courts on Mount Olympus did not have such floors either. Or better to say, "Minton's encaustic-tileless courts," for surely Herbert Minton's Staffordshire, which adorned the floors of the capitol buildings in Washington, had not found their way to those airy heights where the angry Zeus reigned.

Or better still, now that Hopkins had the spotlight and was off on his tear, why not speak of those "vulcanized-india-rubberless courts." Ah, *that* "would strike a keynote at once and bespeak attention. And if the critics said those things did not belong to the period you would have (as you have now with *domeless*) the overwhelming answer, that you never said they did but the contrary, and that Prometheus, who was at once a prophet and as a mechanician more than equal to Edison and the Jablochkoff candle and the Moc-main Patent Lever Truss with self-adjusting duplex gear and attachments." He had meant to say just that: "that they had not got those improvements on Olympus and that the author did not intend that they should. But if you cannot see your way to this 'frank' treatment and are inclined to think that fault might be found with domeless, then remember that that fault is found *in your first line*." And then he added, by way of apology, that the truth was that he was in a "griggish mood" just now, what with the Christmas holidays upon him.

Hopkins the wit, along with Hopkins the Anglican, Hopkins the Catholic, Hopkins the Jesuit, Hopkins the Victorian, Hopkins the scholar and poet, a man intent finally on the one thing necessary: a man clothed in black soutane, an oddity no doubt in Victorian society, becoming all he could be as he burned within with what his mentor Walter Pater had in another context called one's own gemlike flame, which for Hopkins was the one One who could satisfy and console him.

"Cloud-puffball," Hopkins's "That Nature is a Heraclitean Fire" begins, as this perennial stargazer and sunset-painter and cloud-watcher observes once more the clouds above him over Dublin. As a young man he had studied clouds along with bluebells, looking for any least sign of God's presence and beauty and order to be found there. And now, just two days shy of his forty-fourth birthday—which would turn out to be his last—he realized with a terrible start that the intense hard looking he had given to gleaning the heavens for signs of God's presence no longer yielded what it had so abundantly twenty or even ten years before. Cloud gleaning is a young man's game, he knew now, and now his eyes were burned and strained with the task of grading hundreds of bad student translations of his beloved Greek masterpieces.

Over and over again Hopkins observed the passing clouds. "Showers, but mostly bright and hot," he wrote one Sunday night in early June 1866:

Clouds growing in beauty at [the] end of the day. In the afternoon a white rack of two parallel spines, vertebrated as so often. At sunset, when the sky had charm and beauty, very level clouds, long pelleted sticks of shade-softened grey in the West, with gold-colour splashed sunset-spot, then more to the South grey rows rather thicker and their oblique flake or thread better marked. Above them on a ground of indistincter grey a drift of spotty tufts or drops, a 'dirty' looking kind of clouds, scud-like, rising, . . . the meadows yellow with buttercups . . . containing white of oxeyes and puff-balls. . . . The map of the sky . . . a rhomboid of grey round-moulded cloud . . . stretching over the sky.[31]

And two weeks later: "Smart showers in the morning with bright between; this cleared till it was very fine, with flying clouds casting shadows on the Wye hills."[32] Or again: "Sunset fine, soft round curdled clouds bathed with fleshy rose-colour in wedges. . . . Then thunder and lightning and then hard rain."[33] On Tuesday, July 17, the very day he clearly saw "the impossibility of staying in the Church of England," he begins by first noting the shapes of clouds. Today they are merely "dull curds-and-whey."[34] It's as telling an anticlimactic vision of nature's gravitas as anything in Eliot's "Ash Wednesday" or "Little Gidding." And just as authentic.

But here, now, on this late July day in 1888, exhausted from grading those mountains of exams and afraid for his eyes, he had walked out from St. Stephen's Green to look up at the skies again for some kind of reprieve, only to find the clouds flaunting themselves once more, showing off, chevying down the heavens like hounds at harriers after their prey. Heaven-roysterers, he called them: swaggering drunkards thronging overhead, the apparent masters of the skies. And between them: shivelights, shards of glassy light deepening the shadows along the roughcast facades of the cottages, brightening and dimming as sunlight cut through the clouds, defining the damask-sharp shadows of elm branches along the walls, as if graffitiing them, then just as quickly disappearing. It was all a speeding up, a fast-forwarding, a kind of time-lapse photography: here, here, and then gone.

And the wind—noisy and boisterous and rude like the clouds themselves—scattering the standing pools of water in the muddy roads before him, beating earth bare as if firing it, then baking the mud and clay created by the heavy rains in this Heraclitean first day of creation, as the soft doughy imprint of thousands of hoof marks and wheel tracks and boot prints turn to crust then dust, as if they themselves were the fuel creating the smoke clouds overhead that— he sees—were never really clouds at all but rather a sign of the world *burning, burning*, as Augustine said of the streets of Carthage. World's

holocaust, and we mortals, all of us, willy-nilly feeding those flames.
Clouds in their crazed Ovidian metamorphoses "flaunting," "chevying,"
thronging," "glittering," "lacing and lancing and pairing. And the wind,
that other bully-boy, roping, wrestling, beating earth bare. And then,
as if that were not enough, squandering, stanching, starching" the very
earth. Ongoing, ceaseless action in a grand, unending, tumbling cycle,
over and over and over, world without end. Amen.

But Hopkins was not yet finished. He went deeper into this med-
itation on death and loss, even as the *Spiritual Exercises* of the Third
Week had encouraged him to do. Yes, and what else? What more? In a
cruel pun, he noted how the idiot winds likewise snuff and quench the
observer observing all of this. And we? We who stood apart as Nature's
"clearest-selvèd spark," we, with our abrupt, not-to-be-reduplicated,
distinctive selves, we, the so-called pinnacle of all Creation and nature's
"bonniest, dearest to her"? Well, we too go up in smoke in the great
bonfire of Creation as it burns drunkenly, merrily on.

All is unselved, untuned, and, just as violin or catgut strings go slack, all
clear voweling lost, so do we, the words themselves as if swallowed, until
"all is an enormous dark / Drowned." How Hopkins's sibilants capture that
distinctiveness. Listen to them pile up in the inscaping of that sheer-off
shivelight, as "Manshape, that shone / Sheer off, disseveral, a star," was
inevitably beat level just like the drying mud marks there in the streets of
Dublin on that July day in the year 1888.

And more: fame too will go the same way, and all—*all*—the names in
the portraits will ultimately be lost. Ten thousand more years, a mere blink
in chthonic time, and most likely even the names of Michelangelo and
Mozart and Dante and Milton and Shakespeare will join Callimachus and
the lost works of the ancients. Thomas Hardy would say the same in "The
Convergence of the Twain," as would old stony-faced Yeats in a poem he
would write half a century later in "Lapis Lazuli," as the world prepares for
yet another beast slouching toward Bethlehem to be born:

On their own feet they came, or on shipboard,
Camel-back, horse-back, ass-back, mule-back,
Old civilisations put to the sword.
Then they and their wisdom went to rack:
No handiwork of Callimachus,
Who handled marble as if it were bronze,
Made draperies that seemed to rise
When sea-wind swept the corner, stands. . . .

Perhaps Yeats would find some bitter consolation in the great return, the consolation of the Gyres, the sense of things falling apart only to begin again. And thus far Hopkins would agree, cold consolation that such a vision of Nietzschean nihilistic gaiety might be to each of us. But in the longer apocalyptic perspective of infinity even that consolation pales.

But there is another answer, and it comes mid-line in the sixteenth of the sonnet's twenty-four lines, and when it comes, it comes unexpectedly, yet with the clarion cry of abrupt exclamation. Here is God's time cutting across the vastness of Darwinian and Lyellian time, which—as Hart Crane also saw—is but a wink in God's eternal eye. In a letter to Coventry Patmore four years earlier, Hopkins had remonstrated with his friend about the nature of the Second Coming. It was an event, he said, as far as he understood the matter, that would be "sudden, surprising, and unforeseen," and when it came it would be "utterly unmistakable, in that differing from his first coming and all other tokens of himself." Like the sudden shock of the Resurrection itself on that first Easter morning, when the women had gone out early to dress their beloved Master's corpse and had witnessed instead a turning of everything on its head, an event that still shakes millions to the core.

No mistaking it, then, the sheer temporal hyperbaton of it. It is the lesson of the nun on the doomed *Deutschland*, seeing something in that storm, there on that smother of sand in the winter of '75 a dozen years gone now, herself a heart's-clarion calling out after her master and Hopkins's. "What a preposterous summer!" he would write Dixon three days after composing his long sonnet. "It is raining now: when is it not? However there was one windy bright day between floods last week: fearing for my eyes, with my other rain of papers, I put work aside and went out for the day, and conceived a sonnet. Otherwise my muse has long put down her carriage and now for years 'takes in washing.' The laundry is driving a great trade now." All that miserable laundry, those piles and piles of student writing to grade—hundreds on hundreds on hundreds by young Irish and Anglo-Irish lads clamoring for a place in the higher educational system, those with their bad Latin and worse Greek, while he turned over his four hundred pounds' salary each year to help keep afloat a university that might well go under at any moment in the great deluge of Anglo-Irish politics and land rents and Home Rule and the sodden bitterness of three hundred years of mismanagement by a government to which most Irish felt no allegiance. Besides which, he feared for his very eyes now, afraid that they might have hemorrhaged with overwork. Worse, he feared he might go mad at times with the strain of it all, especially as he began counting up his Oxford classmates who were leaving the priesthood and the Church now, or—despairing—simply walking off the stern of ferries in the straits between Dover and Calais, down, down, and down. . . .

Well, no matter now, he still had something he could hold on to: a promise, a consolation, the very thing that had driven a wedge between him and his family, and that had once pushed him to the extreme of telling his brother Lionel—who in his eighty-plus years would never understand why his older brother had become a Catholic, and worse, gone over to those despised Jesuits—to please stop writing him, though they had managed to call a truce on that one and agreed to disagree. Well, he had turned his hand to the plow and he would not look back. Something out there kept beckoning, most days only faintly, like the light from a winter star or a distant beacon. Still, it was something as certain to him as anything he cared for, and for which he was paying the price.

"How to keep," he had written six years earlier, crisping the voices of St. Winifred's maidens,

is there ány any, is there none such, nowhere known some, bow
or brooch or braid or brace, láce, latch or catch or key to keep
Back beauty, keep it, beauty, beauty, beauty, . . . from vanishing away?[35]

Then too he had come close to despair, until—in an instant—the solution had come home to him. No human answer, then as now, but God's. "O why are we so haggard at the heart," he'd asked then. Why

so care-coiled, care-killed, so fagged, so fashed, so cogged, so cumbered,
When the thing we freely fórfeit is kept with fonder a care,
Fonder a care kept than we could have kept it. . . .[36]

And so here again, in the great Mosaic/Pauline/Johannine *Deus ex machina* resolution of Hopkins's last hurrah. Who are you? the shepherd fronting forked lightning had asked the figure in the burning bush, and the answer had come back: "*I AM.*" And again: who *are* you, they had demanded of Christ, and he too had answered, "*I AM.*" And St. Paul, addressing the community at Corinth, having seen at least once into the core of a great mystery, one that had flattened him on the road to Damascus, naked lightning instantaneously, unequivocally striking, as Hopkins had been struck by a similar conversion experience twenty years earlier, on another July day, on a reading holiday with two Oxford companions, the realization of what he had to do coming home to him—as he remembered—"all in a minute."

"Now I am going to tell you a mystery," Paul had written to his little congregation at Corinth with the certitude of the mystic who had come up against nothing less than the brilliance of the resurrected Christ. "We are not all going to fall asleep," he explained, meaning not everyone would die as they expected. "But," he insisted, "we *are* all going to be

changed. Instantly. In the wink of an eye, when the last trumpet sounds.
The trumpet IS going to sound," he assured them, "and then the dead
will be raised imperishable, and we shall be changed, because this
perishable nature of ours must put on imperishability. This *mortal* nature
must put on immortality" (1 Cor. 15:51–53, NJB).

"In a flash, at a trumpet crash," Hopkins has it, all those scurrying
verbs giving way to the verb *to be,* as now—in a nanosecond—we
take on God's own life. No evolution or devolution, no waiting in
groaning expectation. Suddenly, finally, unmistakably, the self of
self, what we mean when we say *"I am,"* will see that it is suddenly
at one with the great *I AM:* "I am all at once what Christ is." And
why? Because of the incredible gift of the Incarnation we have
been offered: of God's breaking in upon the world—"between pied
mountains"—to share his life with us, in his deigning to become
"what I am": man.

So, yes, "this Jack, joke, poor potsherd," this eccentric, this failure
by the world's standards, sent to mend this or that or the other in one
parish or school or university as best he could, this throwaway, this
matchwood flaring up for a moment before going out, yet careful to
match in his own life the life of his ever downwardly mobile Master, this
immortal diamond *is* immortal diamond.

Forty years ago, writing feverishly in a tiny apartment in Flushing,
Long Island, while I rocked my infant son (now a Jesuit) with my foot
as he looked up at me writing there, I saw that no one but the one
on Mount Sinai or the Christ of John's Gospel had ever given greater
force to the simple preterite the way Hopkins managed to do here: that
simple *IS* and *I am* resounding with affirmation down the years. Let it
all burn away. Still, something, something hard and permanent and
magnificent, remains in the world-wielding wildfire of existence, not
because we have earned it, Hopkins understood, but because it has been
given to us by the great lover he tried over the years to tell us about in
music, word, homily, and gesture.

"I will now go to bed," a weary Hopkins wrote Bridges from the town of Fort William in the shadow of Ben Nevis in the highlands of Scotland, where that weekend he was assisting the local parish priest. It was a Saturday night, three weeks after writing his poem, which had been met—Bridges had told him—with stunned puzzlement by the Reverend Dixon *and* himself, the two men Hopkins had hoped would get what he was after. Well, tomorrow morning he would rise up and try again, this time from the pulpit of the local church, trying to put "plainly to a Highland congregation of MacDonalds, MacIntoshes, MacKillops, and the rest what I am putting not at all so plainly to the rest of the world, or rather"—since he had no other audience—"to you and Canon Dixon."

Plainly. So be it. If only, Bridges had insisted, Hopkins would read more, his eccentric and difficult style might in time become more Miltonic and manly and plainspoken, more like . . . like his own. But, Hopkins shot back, would more reading in the Greeks and Romans really make any difference? After all, he'd distilled "a great deal of early Greek philosophical thought" in his sonnet, but "the liquor of the distillation," he reminded Bridges, hadn't tasted "very Greek," had it? And so it had always been with him: the "effect of studying masterpieces" only made him "admire and do otherwise." So it is finally with "every original artist to some degree" and on him to "a marked degree." And refining his singularity, Hopkins smiled, was surely not what Bridges wanted from his friend?

It would be his last sonnet using codas *alla bernesco.* "Spelt from Sybil's Leaves"—which had taken the better part of two years to complete— had been a fourteen-liner with eight stresses to the line. It was the longest Petrarchan sonnet probably ever written, he'd crowed, and it had served as one great departure, just as this extraordinary palinode had answered his private Inferno with its glimpse of a Paradiso. After this, in the months remaining to him, it would be a matter of diminuendos, quiet summations, lonely cries, dustings off of one's hat and a final fond farewell, Lenten preparations as it were for his own early death from typhoid.

In those last months, as the clock finally ran out, Bridges would still not get it, would in fact—much as he later regretted it—burn two of his friend's last letters to him in what turned out to be a prelude to the holocaust of his own letters to Hopkins, once he had them back in his possession. One might conceive a sonnet in an afternoon, but that was only the tip, the distillation, the flowering, of what had taken years to honeycomb and prepare. So Hopkins would explain to Bridges again at the end. And so, if in his lagging lines Bridges missed "The roll, the rise, the carol, the creation," better to blame it on Hopkins's winter world. Still, even now, he managed to yield up a great secret, for his final song is, in fact, made up of sighs: sighs of loss, yes, but sighs too of love.

And not his sighs only, but the sighs of the Father, and of the Son, and the Holy Spirit, in this microcosmic re-creation of what he had come to understand in his own long meditations on the Ignatian *Principle and Foundation*: the threefold fission/fusion that lay at the heart of the Mystery of the Trinity. *They* knew, *they* understand, *they* had placed him where he was now, as now he offered Bridges not his explanation for whatever he had managed to compose in the moments left him after doing what he had been sent to do. No, not his explanation, Bridges had to understand, but the Triune God's in this, their final sighing: his and his Beloved's.

3
THE FRANCISCAN HEARTS OF HOPKINS
AND MERTON

September. 1938. A cold, gray rainy fall day in Manhattan. Tom Merton, twenty-three, is studying in a small room on West 114th Street for his doctorate in English literature at Columbia University. The dark clouds of war are already looming over Europe and the Far East and Merton knows it is just a matter of time before his draft invitation arrives and he will, as he sardonically notes, receive "a piece of metal with my number on it . . . so as to help out the circulation of red-tape that would necessarily follow the disposal of my remains."[37] He understands too well that in the larger scheme of things he does not matter, that his "likes or dislikes, beliefs or disbeliefs" mean absolutely nothing "in the external, political order." That, whatever his particular and unique, never-to-be-repeated consciousness might register, he means nothing to the overall welfare of the state. He is an individual, ironically, in a world in which the individual has ceased to count. And so, if New York is gray, the world is even grayer.

And then he picks up a book, a modest thing. It's a biography written by the Jesuit priest and scholar G. F. Lahey, published eight years earlier, about another Jesuit priest, scholar, and poet who died half a century before whose name was Gerard Manley Hopkins. Merton had already been attracted to Hopkins by some of his poems, but now he learns that Hopkins, raised as an Anglican, and a brilliant student at Balliol College, Oxford, converted to Catholicism at about the age Merton is now. And because he has been thinking of writing his dissertation on Hopkins, he dips into Lahey's biography and discovers that Hopkins, under the influence of John Henry Newman, himself a convert, took the bold step—against the advice of his Oxford dons and his own family's wishes—of becoming a Roman Catholic.

And then, as Merton himself tells the story, "All of a sudden something began to stir within me, something began to push me, to prompt me. It was a movement that spoke like a voice. 'What are you waiting for?' it said. 'Why are you sitting here? Why do you still hesitate? You know what you ought to do? Why don't you do it?'"[38] Uncomfortable with this rude, forceful intrusion, he says he began stirring in his chair. "I lit a cigarette," then "looked out the window at the rain," trying "to shut the voice up. 'Don't act on your impulses,' I thought. This is crazy. This is not rational. Read your book.'"

He began reading again, but the voice only grew all the more insistent. "It's useless to hesitate any longer," it seemed to be saying. "Why don't you get up and go?" And then, he confesses, "I could bear it no longer. I put down the book, and got into my raincoat, and started down the stairs. I went out into the street. I crossed over, and walked along by the gray wooden fence, towards Broadway, in the light rain. And then everything inside me began to sing."

With that, he walked over to the stone presbytery at Corpus Christi and asked to speak with the pastor, Father Ford, who happened, he was told, to be out. But, as Merton was leaving, he saw Fr. Ford walking down the street toward him, and he asked him if he could talk to him. The priest invited him into the presbytery and they sat in the parlor. Then, just like that, Merton told him bluntly that he wanted to become a Catholic. With that, the priest gave him three books to read and arranged for Merton to return for instruction two evenings a week.

Since he'd been baptized as an infant in Prades, France, he was provisionally baptized again at Corpus Christi on November 18, 1938, in the presence of four of his closest friends, three of whom were Jewish: Bob Lax, Sy Freedgood, and Bob Gerdy. The fourth, who stood in as his godfather, was Ed Rice, the one Catholic among them. Then, for the first time in his life, Merton entered a confessional and, worried that he was about to shock the priest who was hearing his confession, recounted his sins, "one by one," as he says, "species by species, as best I could, I tore out all those sins by their roots, like teeth." Some of them, he added, were hard to confess, but he did. And, while he had attended Mass at Corpus Christi back in August, he had had to watch while the others walked up to the steps of the altar to receive Communion.

But this time was different, he explained. This time he "entered into the everlasting movement of that gravitation which is the very life and spirit of God . . . goodness without end," certain that the Lord was calling out to him from some immense depth. It was of necessity a depth that he would—like Hopkins before him—continue to explore for the rest of his life, up until the very end and the very beginning of an even newer, fuller life.

One of the central concepts Merton seems to have picked up from his reading of Hopkins was the Jesuit's fascination with the divine mystery of the world around him. But what does the word *mystery* mean here? Are we not all at times fascinated with the world around us? By the majesty and awe of it? A panorama of the cascading waters of Niagara Falls or the white waters of the Colorado River, or the Rocky Mountains or the Maine coast at sunrise or sunset—various versions of the American Sublime—would surely catch our attention. Look at the poetry of Wallace Stevens, for example, or Frost, or the Passaic Falls just across the river in Paterson, as William Carlos Williams presents them, or Emily Dickinson's New England, or Walt Whitman's America or the Big Sur of California's Robinson Jeffers. There surely was a mystery of sorts.

But for Hopkins and Merton, as for Flannery O'Connor and Teilhard de Chardin, something more needed to be added, and that was the dimension of the sacramental vision, the sense in which the divine manifests itself in all of Creation, no matter how grand or how small. It was something that both Hopkins and Merton as spiritual seekers searched for in the things before them, in a world where, as Flannery O'Connor reminds us, even the meanest of trees might shine in a radiant light.

What was it Merton found in Hopkins so much so that he desired to follow Hopkins not only by becoming a Catholic, but by joining a religious community that he might more fully comprehend what had been given to him as an act of grace? "Thou mastering me / God," Hopkins's great ode "The Wreck of the Deutschland" begins. And there it is, the opening salvo, the overture, as it were, to the young (thirty-one-year-old) Jesuit scholastic's understanding of what he had been sent forth to do.

What was that, if not the need to proclaim the fact that his Lord and Master, Christ, *Ipse*, is—with the Father and the Spirit—worthy of all praise as the Creator whose designs are so often beyond our immediate understanding? How else to understand this God, Merton knew in following Hopkins, than as the one whose designs are finally glimpsed and somehow understood through patience and prayer, when at last the larger picture reveals itself, and we are left with, indeed surprised by, a sense of wonder, awe, and—yes—joy?

Here, then, is Merton, awakening to an Easter morning on the monastery grounds of Gethsemani in Kentucky: "Today was the prophetic day, the first day of the real shining spring . . . , the day of the year when spring became truly credible. Freezing night, but cold bright morning, and a brave, bright shining of sun that is new, and an awakening in all the land, as if the earth were aware of its capabilities!"[39]

In what follows, with that Franciscan heart of his, he notes that out in the field the woodchuck that had burrowed itself underground for its long winter's nap has come out of the dark again this Easter Sunday, "after three months or so of sleep, and at that early hour when it was still freezing. I thought he had gone crazy. But the day proved him right and me wrong." And as the hours pass and the morning becomes "more and more brilliant," Merton can feel the Pentecostal brilliancy of the sun getting more and more into his own blood. And then it dawns on him again, that this is our mission. This is why we humans are here, for "the earth cannot feel all this. We must. But living away from the earth and the trees we fail them." It is we, he underscores, "who are absent from the wedding feast."

Here, again, we come face-to-face with the young Hopkins and his discovery of scholastic theology—and above all, the influence of the medieval Franciscan friar John Duns Scotus, whose writings added to the young Jesuit's Romantic sensibility and understanding of the particular mark of everything in God's ongoing creation, the *haecceitas*—the "thisness"—of each and every thing. It was this insight, which Hopkins began to think of as "inscape," that found such dazzling expression in his condensed sonnet "Pied Beauty."

What helps bind Merton and Hopkins together is what I like to call "the Francis effect": that profound sense in St. Francis of his love for God's world, something to be celebrated always and everywhere, in all seasons, in both the most mundane, if you will, and in the most spectacular aspects of nature. "Praised be You my Lord with all Your creatures," Francis sang,

> especially Sir Brother Sun,
> Who is the day through whom You give us light.
> And he is beautiful and radiant with great splendor,
> Of You Most High, he bears the likeness.

> Praised be You, my Lord, through Sister Moon and the stars,
> In the heavens you have made them bright, precious and fair.

Praised be You, my Lord, through Brothers Wind and Air,
And fair and stormy, all weather's moods,
by which You cherish all that You have made.
Praised be You my Lord through Sister Water,
So useful, humble, precious and pure.
Praised be You my Lord through Brother Fire,
through whom You light the night
and he is beautiful and playful and robust and strong.

Praised be You my Lord through our Sister,
Mother Earth
who sustains and governs us. . . .

Yet it goes deeper than that, for what Francis's insight into the inscape of things revealed in time was nothing less than Christ himself, in this case inscaping his wounds on his beloved Francis. "Joy fall to thee, father Francis," Hopkins wrote two-thirds of the way through "The Wreck of the Deutschland," as he meditated on the ultimate sacrifice those five Franciscan nuns, exiles from their own homeland, all meeting their Lord on this terrible winter's day, reenacting the five wounds of the crucifixion in their own bodies now: joy to Francis, as inscape indwelt for so long became now pure Lovescape:

> Drawn to the Life that died;
>   With the gnarls of the nails in thee, niche of the lance, his
>   Lovescape crucified
>   And seal of his seraph-arrival! and these thy daughters
>   And five-livèd and leavèd favour and pride,
>   Are sisterly sealed in wild waters,
> To bathe in his fall-gold mercies, to breathe in his all-fire glances.

"Man is created to praise, reverence, and serve God our Lord, and by this means to save his soul." Thus the underlying *Principle and Foundation* of the *Spiritual Exercises*. And, Ignatius added, "The other things on the face of the earth are created for man that they may help him in prosecuting the end for which he is created. From this it follows that man is to use them as much as they help him on to his end, and ought to rid himself of them so far as they hinder him as to it." God gives us a world of splendor and immensity, and it is our privilege and responsibility as conscious beings to acknowledge that bounty and to praise the Creator for all he has given us. God, the Grand Designer and Creator: beyond change, but who paradoxically underwrote the dancing kaleidoscopic flux that was (and is) the world at each and every moment, a world where all things interacted in imitation of the Trinitarian three in one—the Utterer, the Uttered, and the Uttering, each perpetually reaching out to the Other, who was always also the One.

"The world," the poet reminds us, is indeed "chárged wíth the grandeur of God." There's a cosmic energy about God's Creation, an electrical charge, both violent and yet violet sweet, ready to instress itself upon us if only we will pay it the attention it deserves. As a poet steeped in the Romantic tradition, and thus permeated by the aliveness of the world around him, Hopkins knew how generation after generation had seared all of nature with our excesses and failings because we continue to insulate ourselves from the living world around us with our own self-bent concerns and virtual nonrealities. But that was not how God saw the world, nor how Christ saw it. With Christ it was a matter of giving and then giving again, of spending himself until he had literally emptied himself.

Of course, Hopkins like Merton was aware of the darker realities of life, the consequences of our neglect and contempt of the earth and all it contains of life, something Hopkins attributed to the crushing effects of our fallen nature on the world itself. In the midst of the earth's beauty, with all its dazzle and delight, was a darker reality, the possibilities of radical destruction we are also heir to in our rush backwards toward what he conceived as our "first slime."

Shortly before his death, Merton, then fifty-three, made a pilgrimage to the Buddhist shrine at Polonnaruwa. As he looked upon the faces of the reclining Buddhas there he was struck, he tells us, by "the silence of the extraordinary faces. The great smiles. Huge and yet subtle. Filled with every possibility, questioning nothing, knowing everything, rejecting nothing, the peace not of emotional resignation . . . that has seen through every question without trying to discredit anyone or anything." He knew that for "the mind that needs well-established positions, such peace, such silence, [could] be frightening."

Looking at those stone faces, he sensed, was like looking at the face of the Mystery itself: "I was suddenly, almost forcibly, jerked clean out of the habitual, half-tied vision of things, and an inner clearness, clarity, as if exploding from the rocks themselves, became evident and obvious. . . ." Here, now, like Hopkins dying of typhoid, whose last words in spite of his suffering, were "I am so happy! I am so happy!" so with Merton. "All problems," he wrote, "are resolved and everything is clear. The rock, all matter, all life, is charged with dharmakaya [the ineffable, the Mystery, where] everything is emptiness and everything is compassion. I don't know when in my life I have ever had such a sense of beauty and spiritual validity running together in one aesthetic illumination." Still, he knew now what he had so obscurely been looking for all his life. What more remained for him to learn he didn't know. But of this he felt sure: that, at last, he had "pierced through the surface and . . . got beyond the shadow and the disguise. The whole thing is very much a Zen garden, a span of bareness and openness and evidence . . . a beautiful and holy vision." It was a vision that began for him in a church on the Upper West Side of New York City, in the shadow of Columbia, back then, a mere blink in the eye of eternity, all those years ago.

4
"THE ONE SANE MILKMAN,
I FEAR"

Growing up in several towns in Oklahoma, John Berryman (1914–1972) served weekdays as an altar boy for Father Boniface Beri, a Benedictine priest, at Holy Family Catholic Church in Anadarko, usually to mostly empty pews.[40] But something about the ritual covered the boy like a woolen blanket, protecting and comforting him, until that was torn from him soon after the family moved to Clearwater, Florida, where his parents hoped to reap the benefits of the land boom there. Too soon, however, harbinger as it was to the Great Depression, Boom turned to Bust. Berryman was John Allyn Smith then, but even the name would change, like everything else. As the economy soured, so did his parents' relationship. Both father and mother began having affairs, and Smith Sr. took to drinking to assuage his own confusion and pain. The boys' mother, Jill Angel, as she called herself, began seeing an older man by the name of John Berryman, who owned the apartments where Jill, John, and his younger brother, Robert, were living.

In what became a surreal scenario, Smith Sr. would abruptly visit the apartment and then just as abruptly leave. The scene repeated itself again and again. There were arguments and accusations between the parents that grew increasingly more alarming. Then, on June 26, 1926, in the alley to the apartment where the two boys were sleeping, Smith Sr. was found dead of a gunshot wound to the chest. The death was ruled a suicide by the detective who investigated the case, but the lack of powder burns on Smith's chest strongly suggests that he was shot by someone else, either his wife or the elder John Berryman. For John Allyn Smith Jr., the scenario took on the nightmare shape of a twentieth-century film noir rendition of *Hamlet*, which helps explain the poet's later obsession with Shakespeare. Time, too, for Jill Angel and her sons to move again, this time north to Queens, New York, along with the elder Berryman, who married Jill Angel three months later, and then, at her insistence, eager as she was to erase the past as much as she could, gave Berryman's surname to both boys.

After that tragic scene "by the sea, by the beautiful sea, you and me" as the song has it, and as Berryman tells us thirty-two years later in "Dream Song 1"—the overture and opening salvo to his epic *Dream Songs*—there "came a departure," after which his life was irrevocably morphed into a world where "nothing fell out as it might or ought."[41] As the boy grew to adulthood, poetry, along with booze and women, became his new woolen comforters. Especially poetry, so that by the time he graduated from Columbia University in 1936, he wanted not only to be like Yeats, the first of all Modernist poets, he wanted to *be* Yeats.

In time, the lure of Yeats, Auden, and Dylan Thomas, together with the Southern Fugitives Allen Tate and John Crowe Ransom, would come to influence the direction of Berryman's own poetry, together with his love of Shakespeare and the classics, as well as Modern Jazz and contemporary African American literature. But under all that was his deep fascination with Hopkins, not only because of Hopkins's combination of the classical and English literary traditions—beginning with Anglo-Saxon verse and on to Chaucer and Shakespeare and Milton and the English Romantics—but also because of the complex ways in which Hopkins had reshaped modern poetry, the words fired through with a sacramental vision of life.

It was Mark Van Doren, Berryman's English professor and mentor at Columbia, who introduced him to Hopkins, who was a hot topic by the mid-1930s, not only as a result of the second publication of Hopkins's poems, but also because his biography was now available along with the publication of his letters, journals, and spiritual writings. All of these had a profound impact on figures ranging from Auden, Stephen Spender, Yvor Winters, David Jones, Wallace Stevens, and Hart Crane, as well as on the younger generation of American poets who were just coming of age at the time, including Elizabeth Bishop, Robert Lowell, and of course Berryman himself.

There was, for example, the impact Hopkins's "The Wreck of the Deutschland" had on the twenty-eight-year-old Robert Lowell. As a Catholic convert, subject to mood swings—"a manic C.O.," as he later referred to himself—Lowell refused to serve in the US Army during World War II, in response especially to what he saw as the murderous Allied bombings of the German Ruhr Region, which targeted German civilians as well as industrial centers and military installations. Foremost among the poems he wrote in response to the killings was "The Quaker Graveyard in Nantucket," which he dedicated to the memory of his cousin Warren Winslow, a naval officer killed, along with 138 other sailors, when their destroyer, the USS *Turner*, exploded off Sandy Hook, New Jersey, on January 3, 1944.

Section 6 of "Quaker Graveyard," titled "Our Lady of Walsingham," provides a somewhat equivocal and macabre resurrection of the corpse of a sailor snagged in the ship's net, an eerie image of the dead raised from the depths only to be returned forever to those same cold and unforgiving waters. Toward the end of the poem, Lowell evokes England's medieval Catholic shrine of Our Lady at Walsingham, where penitents once removed their shoes to walk the final mile over the stony path to their destination. For nearly half a millennium, thousands of pilgrims, among them English kings, came here and to the Carmelite monastery built on the site. Then, in 1538, Henry VIII razed the monastery along with the statue of Our Lady, thinking in that way to erase the Catholic memory dating back to 1061, when the Virgin Mary appeared to a holy woman; in fact, devotion to Our Lady of Walsingham continued (and continues) to live on in the faith of Catholics, Anglo and Roman both.

Moreover, just as "Quaker Graveyard" mourns the moral deformation of the Quakers' original pact with nature by latter-day Nantucket Quakers who—as Melville tells us in *Moby Dick*—earned a reputation as some of the most avid hunters and killers of whales, so Hopkins mourns the dissolution of the Catholic monasteries by Henry VIII, who forsook his Catholic faith when it interfered with his marrying whom and when he decided. For there was a time, Hopkins reminds us in "The Loss of the Eurydice" (April 1878), when English pilgrims marked the very Milky Way as their star-studded guide to Mary's shrine at Walsingham.

In the "Eurydice," Hopkins likewise mourned the death of those who drowned when *HMS Eurydice* sank off the southern coast of England, near where Hopkins spent his summers as a young man. "Surely," Hopkins wrote, troubled by the havoc Henry had wrought in suppressing a faith that had flourished for more than a millennium,

> I need to deplore it,
> Wondering why my master bore it,
> The riving off that race
> So at home, time was, to his truth and grace
>
> That a starlight-wender of ours would say
> The marvellous Milk was Walsingham Way.[42]

Just so, the anonymous "Lament for Our Lady's Shrine at Walsingham," an ancient ballad Hopkins must have known, "Bitter was it, O to view

/ The sacred vine," where now only grass grows, and where once "the walls of Walsingham / So stately did show."[43]

Word begets word, as text begets text. For Hopkins, there was also Milton's "Lycidas" to ponder. "Lycidas," in the tradition of the classical pastoral, honors the death of Edward King, a fellow Cambridgian and Puritan like Milton, a young man of faith with so much promise who drowned in the Irish Sea in August 1637 and whose body, like those of Hopkins's Franciscan nuns and Lowell's Winslow cousin, was never recovered. "Wash far away, where're thy bones are hurl'd," the twenty-eight-year-old Milton laments: "Whether beyond the stormy Hebrides, / Where thou perhaps under the whelming tide / Visit'st the bottom of the monstrous world."

Yet in spite of the loss of Edward King, who is with God now, so too is the spirit of that lost nun with Christ, so that Hopkins can call upon her to "Remember us in the roads, the heaven-haven of the reward." Milton, too, reminds us that while Lycidas has "sunk low" in death, like the sun which sinks in the west only to rise again in the east, so his friend has "mounted high / Through the dear might of him that walk'd the waves" to hear now "the unexpressive nuptial song / In the blest kingdoms meek of joy and love."

Much more could be said of Hopkins's influence on the young Lowell, but let us turn now to the complex triangulation of Hopkins, Lowell, and Berryman as this influenced Berryman's own "Homage to Mistress Bradstreet," written seven years after "Quaker Graveyard." In Berryman's poem, in fact, we go further back in time than either the tragedies of the *Turner* or the *Eurydice* or even Melville's *Pequod*: back to the *Arbella*, part of the Winthrop Fleet that brought a company of pilgrims, among them Anne Bradstreet, North America's first poet, to a brave New World.

The drowned sailor: a striking image of everything human washed under, obliterated by a force with which there is no reckoning. Here is Berryman, in the final line of stanza six and all of seven of his homage to his fantastical Mistress Bradstreet. After weeks sailing across the

Atlantic in the autumn of 1630, a crossing that witnessed the death of a number of passengers from various sicknesses, the *Arbella* finally makes landing in the New World. But on that very day, young Henry Winthrop, having survived the perilous crossing, spies a canoe in an inlet and volunteers to swim out to retrieve it. And here is Berryman, employing an extended parenthesis that rises and rises, only to finally collapse, mimicking the death of youth facing the promise of the new:

And the day itself he leapt ashore young Henry Winthrop

(delivered from the waves; because he found
off their wigwams, sharp-eyed, a lone canoe
across a tidal river,
that water glittered fair & blue
& narrow, none of the other men could swim
and the plantation's prime theft up to him,
shouldered on a glad day
hard on the glorious feasting of thanksgiving) drowned.[44]

There it is, Berryman tells us, thinking of his own hallucinatory reaching out for a lovely woman three centuries dead: all that promise, all that young vigor and courage, in an instant quashed.

So, too, with Hopkins in the sixteenth stanza of the "The Wreck of the Deutschland," where a young sailor—as in one of those Saturday matinee movie scenes where the damsel is rescued by the hero at the last moment from an oncoming locomotive in what Berryman called those "Saturday rescues"—attempts to come to the rescue of a woman in distress, only to end up a corpse, head gone, the body swinging back and forth like some grotesque pendulum from the side of the ship:

One stirred from the rigging to save
The wild woman-kind below,

> With a rope's end round the man, handy and brave—
>   He was pitched to his death at a blow,
> For all his dreadnought breast and braids of thew:
> They could tell him for hours, dandled the to and fro
>   Through the cobbled foam-fleece, what could he do
> With the burl of the fountains of air, buck and the flood of the wave?[45]

Here is Lowell in "Quaker Graveyard," recalling Hopkins, as well as his own New England forebears, Thoreau (remembering a grisly shipwreck off Cape Cod) and Melville:

> A brackish reach of shoal off Madaket—
> The sea was still breaking violently and night
> Had steamed into our North Atlantic Fleet,
> When the drowned sailor clutched the drag-net. Light
> Flashed from his matted head and marble feet,
> He grappled at the net
> With the coiled, hurdling muscles of his thighs:
> The corpse was bloodless, a botch of reds and whites,
> Its open, staring eyes
> Were lustreless dead-lights
> Or cabin-windows on a stranded hulk
> Heavy with sand. We weight the body, close
> Its eyes and heave it seaward whence it came,
> Where the heel-headed dogfish barks its nose
> On Ahab's void and forehead; and the name
> Is blocked in yellow chalk.[46]

Again, text begets text. T. S. Eliot's *The Waste Land*, which both Lowell and Berryman well knew, evokes yet another drowned sailor, this one Phlebas the Phoenician, a fortnight dead, as the body enters the dreaded whirlpool, Le Neant, the Void, attentive to nothing now, neither "the cry of gulls" nor "the deep sea swell" nor the things of this world that preoccupied the Phoenician in his time as it did Eliot the banker in his, the shadow of the man evoking all that "profit and loss."

Moreover, Berryman borrows Hopkins's eight-line stanzas, where the ending of the opening line returns at the ending of the stanza's final line in a kind of great return, as omega returns to alpha. Hopkins is far stricter in the mathematical precision of his lines, where the rhyme scheme is consistently *ababcbca*, a movement out, then further out again, before returning to the beginning, a form that seems to reflect Hopkins's long meditation on the great *De Processu*, where the Word within the cosmos unfolds, only to return at the end to its Origin, in the process enriching (and celebrating) the meaning of things over and over again.

It's a pattern reinforced by the meter itself, which begins with a two-stress line, followed by a three-stress, then a four-stress, then back to a three-stress line. Then the first four lines are expanded, first by two five-stress lines, followed by a temporary fall-back to a four-stress, before taking wing in a final six-stress crescendo. This is the pattern throughout the first part of the poem, which focuses on Hopkins's own turning to God under a fiery instress. The pattern of part 2 parallels part 1, except that the first line of each stanza expands to a full three stresses.

But what makes Hopkins's lines so vital and electrically charged is his use of sprung rhythm, in which each foot contains one stress, and one stress only, whether the foot is made up of one syllable, two (what we call a trochee), three (a dactyl), four (a first paeon), or occasionally even more syllables. There, then, in the opening salvo of the ode, are the strong stresses native to the ancient Anglo-Saxon alliterative tradition, stresses inherent in the words themselves, a fair number of them that Hopkins marked, so that we can better read the poem as he intended:

Thóu mástering me   2
Gód! giver of bréath and bréad;   3
Wórld's stránd, swáy of the séa;   4

Lórd of líving and déad;   3
Thou hast bóund bónes and véins in me, fástened me flésh,   5
And áfter it álmost únmade, whát with dréad,   5
Thy dóing: and dóst thou tóuch me afrésh?   4
Óver agáin I féel thy fínger and fínd thée.   6

But then Hopkins's radically innovative system of stress scansion was (and often continues to be) met with confusion. Hopkins's Jesuit editors at *The Month* who read the marked manuscript of "Deutschland" that Hopkins sent them had no understanding of what he was up to, and even his friends—Robert Bridges included—did not know what to make of this new music, if indeed it was music at all. For what Hopkins had wrought certainly did not sound like Wordsworth or Keats or Tennyson or even Swinburne.

The closest parallel Bridges could find to a poet who was doing anything like what Hopkins was doing was that strange American self-styled bard across the Atlantic, Walt Whitman. But when Bridges broached this suggestion to Hopkins, Hopkins balked. Whitman, Hopkins insisted, was too expansive, ranging freely all over the page, like the Grand Canyon or the Great Plains. His was a poetry approximating prose, whereas Hopkins had calculated all his poetic movements and was ready to defend them with a Pythagorean accuracy.

It would take subsequent generations to begin to appreciate what Hopkins had achieved. Not Bridges's generation, or even the next— Pound and Eliot and William Carlos Williams, though Hart Crane, mystical note-catcher that he was, and thanks to Yvor Winters, who lent Crane his 1918 volume of Hopkins's poems, did catch something of their splendor and majesty. Instead, it would be Auden and Spender and David Jones, and later Bishop and Lowell and Berryman, who realized what Hopkins, despite the odds in favor of his simply being obliterated by time and neglect, had given the world. What a splendid gift it was.

Berryman's "Homage to Mistress Bradstreet," published in 1956, clearly mimes the stanzaic pattern of Hopkins's "Deutschland," with some significant riffs. "Bradstreet" is a long and complex poem, equal parts announcement and confession, in which the speaker evokes the resurrected spirit of the seventeenth-century poet Anne Bradstreet to address her directly, to lend her a sensitive ear, which soon turns into an attempt to seduce her. This was in fact a disturbing psychological pattern in Berryman: the demonstration of a sense of professional mastery, something the poem demonstrates over and over, but complicated by a strategy of coming to a vulnerable woman's rescue to bed her.

Sadly, Berryman crossed this line as a teacher and confidante several times, and the poem is as much a confession of this skewed sense of psychic mastery and of infidelity to his wife, Eileen Simpson, as it is an announcement of his mastery of a poetic form. Consider, for example, the opening salvo of the first of the fifty-seven stanzas of "Bradstreet," a poem one and a half times as long as Hopkins's "Deutschland":

The Governor your husband lived so long
moved you not, restless, waiting for him? Still,
you were a patient woman. —
I seem to see you pause here still:
Sylvester, Quarles, in moments odd you pored
before a fire at, bright eyes on the Lord,
all the children still.
"Simon . . ." Simon will listen while you read a Song.

The poem opens with the poet addressing, not the five dead nuns who perished in that winter storm, as Hopkins's does, but rather the dead Anne Bradstreet, restlessly waiting for her husband to join her in death. Quickly, though, the poet raises the woman back to a momentary life of a sort, watching her as she reads two long-forgotten English poets who influenced her, both miserable poets, as far as Berryman is concerned: Joshua Sylvester (1563–1618) and Francis Quarles (1592–1644). The poet also sees Anne, good Puritan that she was, praying the Psalms to her children in the evenings as she prepares them for bed. Note especially the repetition of the word "still," repeated three times in eight lines, in each instance a line ending, and each time followed by the stillness of a pause. First, there's still, as in "nevertheless." Then there's still, in the sense of an ongoing activity. And, finally, there is the stillness of the children as they fall asleep. But there's another sense of still as well, as in the stillness of death, of someone frozen in time, whom the poet-necromancer now raises back to life.

There's also the couplet in lines five and six, where "poured" chimes with "Lord." And the end rhymes of the first and last lines of the stanza, where "long" rhymes with "Song," reminding us that we are about to embark on an extended song. That leaves just one line without a rhyme to complement it: line three, which ends with the word "woman," a line without a counterpart or mate. And it is Berryman who will strive to fill that role, unsuccessfully, of course, since death will have the last word. What we have, then, is a rhyming pattern that goes like this: abxbccba. Other stanzas will deviate even more from this paradigm in terms of unrhymed lines. Occasionally, one finds a stanza in which the rhyme scheme is complete, if we allow for half-rhymes, as in stanza three (abcbaaca) where air (oxygen) rhymes with air (as in a melodic duet), then "year" completing the couplet, and finally "disappear," and where "see" rhymes with "we," and "it" pararhymes with "not." But mostly there's a jazzlike riff or incompleteness about the stanzas: abxxccba, say, or axxbccba, as in the final stanza.

O all your ages at the mercy of my loves
together lie at once, forever or
so long as I happen.
In the rain of pain & departure, still
Love has no body and presides the sun,

and elf's from silence melody. I run.
Hover, utter, still,
a sourcing whom my lost candle like the firefly loves.

Here, at the poem's conclusion, is that "still" again, as Bradstreet returns to the stillness of death, even as Berryman implores her spirit to hover over his poem and remain a sourcing, with the realization too that the candle of inspiration and his own life must flicker and go out.

There are also the similarities of language and syntax in Hopkins and Berryman to consider, especially the strong verb-centered diction both employ. Consider both poets' descriptions of the effects of the wintry sea storm on the passengers of both the *Deutschland* and the *Arbella*. Here is Hopkins, as his ship makes its way through the North Sea before it founders off the coast of England:

> Into the snows she sweeps,
> Hurling the haven behind,
> The Deutschland, on Sunday; and so the sky keeps,
> For the infinite air is unkind,
> And the sea flint-flake, black-backed in the regular blow,
> Sitting Eastnortheast, in cursèd quarter, the wind;
> Wiry and white-fiery and whirlwind-swivellèd snow
> Spins to the widow-making unchilding unfathering deeps.

Here, then, is Berryman, describing the two-week crossing of the Arbella as it makes its way to the New World:

> Strange ships across us, after a fortnight's winds
> unfavouring, frightened us;
> bone-sad cold, sleet, scurvy; so were ill
> many as one day we could have no sermons;
> broils, quelled; a fatherless child unkennelled; vermin
> crowding & waiting: waiting.

Noteworthy, too, is Berryman's "unfavouring" and "unkennelled," echoing Hopkins's "unchilding" and "unfathering." In both poems there's an explosive force as the language mimics the violence and instress of nature on the misery-soaked passengers—and, by extension, on us. But where the storm eventually lifts in Hopkins following the deaths of the passengers, including all five nuns, death seems to win out as Berryman's mistress returns to the void out of which the poet has lifted her, at least for the duration of the poem.

Again and again, Berryman found himself returning to Hopkins's vital sprung rhythm and language, even as he struggled against the deeper, spiritual significance of that same spiritual impulse, spiraling instead ever deeper into the giddy nihilism manifested in so many of his 77 *Dream Songs* (1964). This tension between word and spirit became a lifelong battle for Berryman, an inner war that took its toll not only on his own health and sanity, but on his family and friends as well. And because it is often hardest for a poet to admit to his deepest influences—for that would be, as Hopkins himself once said, like "telling secrets"—Berryman found himself aligned in many ways with that brilliant, roaring alcoholic Welshman, Dylan Thomas, dead at thirty-nine, whose last hours Berryman himself witnessed in a New York hospital.[47]

There were other influences on Berryman as well: Horace, Dante, Georg Trakl, and Rainer Maria Rilke, as well as Shakespeare and the Elizabethan and Jacobean playwrights whom he studied assiduously. And there was the generation that preceded him: Yeats, Edward Arlington Robinson, Robert Frost, Stephen Crane and Hart Crane, William Carlos Williams, Wallace Stevens, Ezra Pound, T. S. Eliot, and Auden, among them. And there were his contemporaries, among them Theodore Roethke, Randall Jarrell, Elizabeth Bishop, Sylvia Plath, and Lowell, with whom he argued back and forth in his poems for a quarter century, and upon whom the *Dream Songs* made a deep and lasting impact. Still, the deepest influence on Berryman, both poetically and spiritually, remained that brilliant failure, Fr. Hopkins, as many of the *Dream Songs* and especially the late poems—

from the "Eleven Addresses to the Lord" through his Opus Posthumous series—demonstrate.

Naturally the path of Hopkins's influence on Berryman was anything but straightforward, especially since Berryman's lifelong wrestling with his frenemy God took such violent twists and turns. Bradstreet reflects this battle, as even the pious Anne struggles to understand why God could have left her face wracked by smallpox, or taken her daughter from her, or allowed those pilgrims seeking to establish a New World order to perish at sea or in the city on the hill that they sought to build against insurmountable odds. Again and again Berryman's alter ego Henry questions who this God really is, and it's a struggle as intense in its own way as Hopkins's wrestling with his God in the sonnets of 1884 and '85.

Consider two of the *Dream Songs*, which speak to each other across the page: DS 237 and DS 238. In the first a couple is caught in the act of adultery by the local KKK and executed where they have been discovered. Henry, aware that he too has been in situations where the same end might conceivably have happened to him, is there to witness their violent deaths:

When in the flashlights' flare the adultering pair
sat up with horror under the crab-apple tree
(soon to be hacked away for souvenirs)
and with their breasts & brains waited, & with ears
while masked & sheeted figures silently—
"Kneel, I—love," he stammered, "and pray," Henry was there.

When four shots snapped, one for the Reverend,
her sick howl, three for her, in the heads, all fatal, and
when her throat is slit so deep the backbone eddies,
her worshipful foolish letters strewn between the bodies,
her tongue & voice-box out, his calling card
tipped up by his left heel, Henry was toward.

But then, in the third stanza, Berryman imagines the preacher and Mrs. Mills chastened, yes, but redeemed and made infinitely wiser by an all-merciful God, as the mistakes humans make are washed away by the reality of what ultimately IS, finally understood, as now the couple enters the celestial choir, their mangled bodies resurrected, singing praise to God:

> When to the smokeless mild celestial air
> they came reproved & forgiven, her soul hurrying after his,
> when bright with wisdom of the risen Lord
> enthroned, they swam toward where what may be IS
> and with the rest Mrs Mills, larynx & tongue restored,
> choiring Te Deum.

But this time, the poet tells us, chillingly, "Henry was not there." It is a vision of the poet yearning after salvation, but seeing it from the standpoint of a hell out of which he cannot escape.

Then, having reached the point where he sees himself damned, Berryman fires back at the Father who seems to have abandoned him, as he was abandoned years before by his own father. In "DS 238," Berryman presents us with "Henry's Programme for God." Why are we even here, Henry wonders, and why

> did we ever come at all,
> consonant to whose bidding? Perhaps God is a slob,
> playful, vast, rough-hewn.

> Perhaps God resembles one of the last etchings of Goya
> & not Valesquez, never Rembrandt, no.
> Something disturbed,
> ill-pleased, & with a touch of paranoia
> who calls for this thud of love from his creatures-O.
> Perhaps God ought to be curbed.

Not only on this planet, I admit, somewhere.
Our only resource is bleak denial or
anti-potent rage,
both have been tried by our wisest. Who was it back there
who died unshriven, daring to see what more
could happen to a painter with such courage?

Just here, then, Berryman turns to the great classical artists Velasquez and Rembrandt, on the positive side of the equation for the ultimate meaning of life, with Goya and Perugino on the other. To make his point, Berryman references Goya's late etchings and paintings, and most probably—though he does not name it specifically—Goya's Saturn eating his son, from his *Proverbios* or *Sueños*, painted when the artist was in his late seventies. In it we do indeed witness a paranoid god frantically ripping a body to pieces—his own son's, it turns out—and devouring it. And then there is Perugino, who, according to Vasari, refused the last sacraments, saying that he would wait to see what more God could possibly have in store for him on the other side of the Great Divide.

"Dream Song 238" was composed in late August of 1966 and is certainly one of Berryman's darkest poems. But then there's "Dream Song 377," composed just four months later, while Berryman was living with his wife and small daughter in Ballsbridge, Dublin. It's one of a number of late poems on the nature of human suffering shared by good and decent people, Hopkins among them. The poem was written at Christmas 1966, and it recalls Hopkins's final years spent in Dublin, "teaching elementary Greek / whilst his mind climbed the clouds." And though Hopkins's life seemed a failure, yet he kept the faith, a faith Henry wishes he might somehow likewise keep. Jonathan Swift also died in Dublin a century and more before Hopkins, Berryman reminds us, a poet who at the end "wandered mad through his rooms & could not speak," a fate not unlike what Berryman feared for himself. But Hopkins, with his eyes on the Milky Way, surely died "A milkman sane," the only poet he knows of, "the one one, I fear," who can claim that ultimate sanity, in spite of the fact that, as Berryman well knew, Hopkins's "name was gone almost," the fame he so richly deserved almost escaping him.

Somehow, though, "Hopkins' credits," Berryman tells us, "while the Holy Ghost / rooted for Hopkins, hit the Milky Way." What Berryman recalls here is a sermon Hopkins delivered on April 25, 1880, the fourth Sunday after Easter, while ministering to his mostly working-class Irish flock at the Jesuit church of St. Francis Xavier in Liverpool. In that sermon, Hopkins reminded his parishioners that Jesus had called the Holy Spirit the Paraclete, the "One who comforts, who cheers, who encourages, who persuades, who exhorts, who stirs up, who urges forward, who calls on."

By way of explaining what a Paraclete was, he offered his congregation a steady stream of brilliant, everyday metaphors—describing things as familiar to them, and unexpected from the mouth of their priest, as a cricket match with all its strategic intricacies. Like the spectators of such a match, the Paraclete was "something that cheers the spirit of man, with signals and with cries, all zealous that he should do something and full of assurance that if he will he can, calling him on, springing to meet him half way, crying to his ears or to his heart: This way to do God's will, this way to save your soul, come on, come on!" So, too, with Hopkins himself, whom Berryman recognized as his own Paraclete: a poet, finally, whose "credits"—as at the end of a film revealing who the true actors are in a now-completed drama—hit the Milky Way.

Yeats, Berryman reminds us, did not die in his own native Ireland, but rather in France, though years after the end of World War II his remains, "they say," were "brought back by a warship & put down." And so with that other great Irishman, James Joyce, buried in Switzerland. But Hopkins, an Englishman who so loved his native England, died here in Dublin from typhoid and is buried in a common grave with his fellow Jesuits in Glasnevin Cemetery, in what Berryman calls this "barbaric and green" country. Or, he asks at the close of the poem, did those tasked with the duty simply "growl 'God's damn' / the lousy Jesuit, canned."

It's that final word, that final judgment, it would seem, that no doubt troubles the reader. In what sense was Hopkins "canned"? An obvious reading is the idiomatic sense of being canned or fired from a job because one is judged unworthy. Or it could mean being dumped unceremoniously in a common grave with his fellow Jesuits as if they were merely canned goods whose time had expired. But Hopkins himself offers us another reading, one that he provides us with in one of his most powerful poems, "Carrion Comfort."

In that untitled poem (the title—in parentheses—later provided by Robert Bridges), left behind by its author like so many others on a loose scrap of paper, the poet seems almost suicidal in his dejection. It begins with the poet fighting against the temptation to simply let go and end it all. "Not," the poem begins,

> I'll not, carrion comfort, Despair, not feast on thee;
> Not untwist — slack they may be — these last strands of man
> In me ór, most weary, cry I can no more. I can;
> Can something, hope, wish day come, not choose not to be.

I can no more, Hopkins writes. The phrase, ironically crying out from the line as an assertion of what the speaker fears he may give way to, recalls some lines from Fr. John Henry Newman, the man who had brought Hopkins into the Church. Newman's "The Dream of Gerontius" is a long meditation spoken by an old man on the point of death. It's a poem, Newman once said, written by accident and subsequently published by accident in 1865, the year before Hopkins's own conversion, in the pages of *The Month*, the same publication that would later reject Hopkins's "Deutschland" and then "The Loss of the Eurydice," which led to Hopkins's decision that, if his own Jesuits would not publish him, then he was through sending his work out. "I can no more," Gerontius cries out,

> for now it comes again,
> That sense of ruin, which is worse than pain,
> That masterful negation and collapse
> Of all that makes me man; as though I bent
> Over the dizzy brink
> Of some sheer infinite descent;
> Or worse, as though
> Down, down for ever I was falling through
> The solid framework of created things,
> And needs must sink and sink
> Into the vast abyss. And, crueller still,
> A fierce and restless fright begins to fill
> The mansion of my soul. And, worse and worse,
> Some bodily form of ill
> Floats on the wind, with many a loathsome curse
> Tainting the hallow'd air, and laughs, and flaps
> Its hideous wings,
> And makes me wild with horror and dismay.
> O Jesu, help! pray for me, Mary, pray!
> Some Angel, Jesu! such as came to Thee
> In Thine own agony. . . .

At the end, mercifully, the dying man's cry is heard and he ultimately finds comfort. So now with Hopkins, calling on Newman yet again, nearly twenty years on. Newman: his own Paraclete, his comforter in difficult times, that gentle man, through his surrogate Gerontius calling out in his distress. Three times in two lines, Hopkins cries out from the depths, insisting that he can do something in the face of despair. He will not follow Gerontius down the road to despair, but, exhausted as he is, continue the fight. He can, "Can something, hope, wish day come, not choose not to be."

Now, eighty years on, Berryman evokes his "one sane milkman" who, despite his apparent failures and near-despair, a man nearly crucified, cries out as Christ did on the cross, "My God! My God!" This is Berryman's Paraclete, then, his comforter, cheering Berryman on, telling him to get up and keep trying, that it is not too late, as hard as things may seem to be. If it is a cat-and-mouse existence for Berryman, as it was for his friends Delmore Schwartz and Randall Jarrell and Theodore Roethke— for all of whom Berryman wrote elegies, some of them extending over half a dozen *Dream Songs* or more—where madness itself seemed to have taken hold, there is instead Hopkins's example, refusing to give in to despair and realizing with a shock that beyond those "darksome devouring eyes" scanning his "bruisèd bones," there's a reason for all this pain. And what is that? That he might be purged of his own clinging ego that still held back from giving himself as he had hoped to, and that, purified through his suffering, as he confesses yet again as he did years earlier in "The Wreck," his

> chaff might fly; my grain lie, sheer and clear.
> Nay in all that toil, that coil, since (seems) I kissed the rod,
> Hand rather, my heart lo! lapped strength, stole joy, would laugh, chéer.
> Cheer whom though? the hero whose heaven-handling flung me, fóot
> tród
> Me? or me that fought him? O which one? is it each one? That night,
> that year
> Of now done darkness I wretch lay wrestling with (my God!) my God.

So, too, with Berryman, enmeshed still after so many years in a life of booze, prone to rage and with an intemperate pride in his poetic achievements. "My tough Songs well in Tokyo & Paris / fall under scrutiny," he half crows, half mocks himself in the opening salvo of *Love & Fame*, in a poem, "Her & It," composed in February 1970, when he was fifty-five:

> My publishers
> very friendly in New York & London
> forward me elephant cheques.
>
> Time magazine yesterday slavered Saul's ass,
> they pecked at mine last year. We're going strong!
> Photographs all over!

His old friend Saul Bellow had just published his Holocaust novel, *Mr. Sammler's Planet*, which was being met with rave reviews and would win the National Book Award for fiction the following year. And just a year earlier Berryman himself had won the same award for his *Dream Songs*. And now he was three-fourths of the way through *Love & Fame*, when in May 1970 he was admitted to St. Mary's psychiatric unit in Minneapolis, under close supervision.

An Episcopal priest who ministered to the most troubled patients at St. Mary's explained to Berryman that he would no longer be able to leave the hospital to teach his classes because Berryman had the insane habit of ordering the taxi that drove him back to the hospital after classes to stop at a local bar so he could refresh himself with five or six stiff drinks before he continued his recovery.

But, the priest told Berryman, he himself would teach Berryman's classes for him while he was in recovery. Once more, Berryman suddenly realized, someone had come to his rescue. Someone, something, had been there for him when he most needed it, when he was most vulnerable, most wounded. It was then that Berryman broke down, sobbing with relief and gratitude.

At this point he saw the possibility of a new direction: to empty himself—inasmuch as he could, given who he was—and turn back to the Father he had rejected and scorned for so long. Out of this experience came "Addresses to the Lord," eleven addresses, in fact, of varying length: songs of praise, astonishment, doubt, confession, all laced with that delicious jazzy humor so characteristic of the man. "Master of beauty, craftsman of the snowflake, / inimitable contriver," the sequence begins, once again echoing the opening of Hopkins's "Deutschland." The Father, his Father, "endower of Earth so gorgeous & different from the boring Moon," he wrote, "thank you for such as it is my gift." Ah, the moon, lately visited by US astronauts who had revealed its empty, desertlike surface, a landscape similar to the desolation of his own interior world.

"You have come to my rescue again & again," he confesses now, "in my impassable, sometimes despairing years. / You have allowed my brilliant friends to destroy themselves / and I am still here, severely damaged, but functioning." Then, veering this way and that, he ended the poem by turning with amazement back to a Creator too large for anyone ever to fully comprehend. He begged only to remain alert now, open to his Master's presence. At last he understood that there were two ends to consider: God's end, God's plan, something starkly contrasted with his own end, which was now more than ever fast approaching. "Whatever your end may be," he wrote,

> accept my amazement.
> May I stand until death forever at attention
> for any your least instruction or enlightenment.
> I even feel sure you will assist me again, Master of insight & beauty.

Love & Fame he would call his new collection of poems. Of course he had Keats's own sonnet in mind when he titled it that. "When I have fears that I may cease to be," Keats had written when he knew that time was running out for him, as now for Berryman:

> Before my pen has glean'd my teeming brain,
>   Before high piled books, in charact'ry,
>   Hold like rich garners the full-ripen'd grain
>   . . . then on the shore
> Of the wide world I stand alone, and think
> Till Love and Fame to nothingness do sink.

What, after all, were love and fame? Those things that he, like so many others, had made life seem worth living? Hopkins had provided one answer to that question. In June 1878, the newly ordained priest had written from Stonyhurst, where he had been teaching, to tell his former teacher Canon Dixon that, though it was unfortunately the case that Dixon had no appreciable and appreciative audience for his poems, he did have in Hopkins at least one reader who understood the beauty of what he'd accomplished.

But no, he corrected himself, there were two: himself and the Master whom they both served. "Fame," he told Dixon, "whether won or lost is a thing that lies in the award of a random, reckless, incompetent judge, the public, the multitude. The only just judge, the only just literary critic, is Christ, who prizes, is proud of, and admires, more than any man, more than the receiver himself can, the gifts of his own making."[48] True fame, thank God, lay in the hands of "a perfectly just, heedful, and wise mind," and that was Christ's.

So, here, in the eighth of his addresses, Berryman acknowledged once again that Fr. Hopkins had got it right. He recalled the scene from Exodus where Moses, atop the sacred mountain, had asked to see the Lord and was granted a sense of God's passing over, so that Moses would see him briefly, but only from behind:

> Then the Lord said, "There is a place near me where you may stand on a rock. When my glory passes by, I will put you in a cleft in the rock and cover you with my hand until I have passed by. Then I will remove my hand and you will see my back; but my face must not be seen."

"Fearful I peer upon the mountain path," Berryman wrote now, "where once Your shadow passed, Limner of the clouds / up their phantastic guesses." Even here, then, with awe and terror and love shadowing him, Berryman could not avoid punning on "guesses" and "dresses," up which he now gazed. And then, with that momentary comic impulse, that nervous stutter of a laugh, out of the way, he could finally say what was really on his mind. "I am afraid," he admitted, to something he had "never until now confessed," that, yes, once again—as he had as a boy serving on an altar in Anadarko, Oklahoma—he had fallen "back in love" with his Father. And so he asks God to do to him what he had done for Hopkins, and so many others, including all those souls struggling in AA with him, to

> Oil all my turbulence as at Thy dictation
> I sweat out my wayward works.
> Father Hopkins said the only true literary critic is Christ.
> Let me lie down exhausted, content with that.

That was what he pleaded for now: the peace that came with writing not for himself or for the pages of *TIME* magazine or the *New York Review of Books* or even the *New York Times*. Like that one sane milkman, whose fame had come posthumously—though as it happened, a thousand times more brilliantly than Hopkins himself must ever have expected—he too hoped from now on to sweat out his writing at God's dictation. Which is what he tried so desperately to do in the year and a half he had left in his last book of poems, the aptly named *Delusions, Etc.*, published after his death in January 1972.

Among these poems one finds his "Opus Dei," a poetic sequence composed in the winter and early spring of '71. There is, too, the brilliant, unfinished novel he worked on that he called—half hopefully, half ironically—*Recovery*. There are also elegies to Trakl and Dylan Thomas and a poem for his baby daughter Sarah, who arrived that June. ("Hello there, Biscuit!" he wrote two weeks after she was born. "You're a better-looking broad / by much than, and your sister's dancing up & down.")[49]

But then, too, there was the poem he composed between 1:15 and 2:15 AM on the morning of May 20 in his room (406) at the Shoreham Motor Inn at 765 Asylum Avenue in Hartford, Connecticut. Here he was, he noted, in "Wallace Stevens' town," near Stevens's old office at the Hartford Accident and Indemnity Company, one of the nation's leading insurance companies, whose downtown offices were only a mile from Stevens's home. He called his thirty-nine-line composition "The Facts & Issues" and confessed that he was weirdly certain that he'd found God there in the room with him. It was, however, a fact that had unsettled him. "I really believe He's here all over this room," he wrote. "He," he noted this time, rather than the familiar "You," and he found that presence terrifying. Still, this was no mere "hypothesis." Yes, God was right there in the room with him! And then he went on, somewhat comforted by the fact that "millions agree with me, or mostly do, / and have done ages of our human time, / among whom were & still are some very sharp cookies."

Well, what was he to do now? Spread the word about what he'd just experienced? "I don't exactly feel missionary about it," he admitted, "though it's very true I wonder if I should." Of course, there were those who would simply dismiss what he was experiencing as a mere delusion. But then he regarded those "boys" just as deluded as himself, though he wasn't just going to say "the hell with them." Part of the problem for him was that he still felt dubious and uneasy about this whole hell thing. Years before—in "Dream Song 56"—he'd signed on with the early theologian Origen's concept of *apocatastasis*: that hell would one day lie empty and that everyone—even the devil—would share in the grace of salvation. After all, there was enough hell here "all right, but elsewhere, after? Screw that." Evil, he had to believe, ended when one died (thank God), while good, he hoped, continued to blaze on.

But what of this Presence in the room with him here, now, in the middle of the night, in a motel room in downtown Hartford? The Presence, he had to believe, was mild, and surely meant him no harm. Yet he also knew he didn't "dare go nearer" It. As for the time he still had here on earth, he confessed he was "Happy to be here / and to have been here / with such lovely ones so infinitely better" than himself. But could he really bear to be happy forever, "for Christ's sake" forever? And yes, it was true that

Christ underwent man & treachery & socks
& lashes, thirst, exhaustion, the bit, for my pathetic & disgusting vices,
to make this filthy fact of particular, long-after,
faraway, five-foot-ten & moribund
human being happy.

Well, he *was* happy. In fact, he was so happy he could scream! But enough was enough! "I can't BEAR ANY MORE," he screamed in capital letters. "Let this be it. I've had it. I can't wait."

Happy. There it is, embedded in the poem itself: Hopkins's own last words, uttered as he lay dying in his own small room on the ground floor of the Jesuit residence there in Dublin, facing St. Stephen's Green: "I am so happy," Hopkins had whispered. And then a second time: "I am so happy." But if Hopkins's final words encapsulated a sense of quiet ecstasy, as if he had just experienced a comforting Presence there in the room with him, a Presence ready to embrace him, Berryman's words expressed equal amounts of fear and extreme exasperation: a sense of psychic exhaustion, waiting now for the journey to be over and done with.

And so it would turn out to be soon enough. On the frigid morning of January 7, 1972, Berryman left his house and wife and two small daughters and walked down to and then across the campus of the University of Minnesota, where he'd taught for the past two decades, then stopped halfway across the walkway that spanned the bluffs over the Mississippi River flowing a hundred feet below. Then he balanced himself on the metal rail, much as another poet whom he had so much admired as a young man had also done. This was Hart Crane, who forty years earlier had balanced himself on the stern rail of the *SS Orizaba* and then plunged into the yawing ocean. Now, on this frozen morning in Minneapolis, Berryman, too, took a moment to wave goodbye to the students hurrying across the bridge, then dropped into the unforgiving void below. He was fifty-seven years old.

For eleven months, with the help of Alcoholics Anonymous, he'd stayed away from booze altogether, often coming to the aid of other alcoholics. And then, just a few days earlier, he'd picked up a bottle of whiskey and started drinking again. On January 5, he scribbled down what would be his last poem. It took the form of a Dream Song, and, in that grotesque comic fashion he had perfected over the years, outlined how he meant to escape the embarrassment of giving lectures he was sure would end this time with his students

> dropping the course,
> the Administration hearing
> & offering me either a medical leave of absence
> or resignation.

Well, he had a better plan, he addressed his wife, Kate. "Kitticat," he wrote, "they can't fire me." The poem was short one line, as if swallowed by the Void.

Fall, he had written years earlier in another Dream Song. Fall was something that had to do intrinsically with grief, something, as he'd said, something "grievy." Hopkins had known that same feeling as well. "Márgarét, áre you grieving," the Jesuit had written once,

> Over Goldengrove unleaving?
> Leáves like the things of man, you
> With your fresh thoughts care for, can you?
> Ah! ás the heart grows older
> It will come to such sights colder
> By and by, nor spare a sigh
> Though worlds of wanwood leafmeal lie;
> And yet you wíll weep and know why.
> Now no matter, child, the name:
> Sórrow's spríngs áre the same.

Nor mouth had, no nor mind, expressed
What heart heard of, ghost guessed:
It ís the blight man was born for,
It is Margaret you mourn for.

The fall of the year, the fall of humankind from its early promise, a fall from a spectacular height. A simple tilt forward, and it was over.

And yet, and yet. Despite his suicide, and the enormous sense of failure that went with that decision and with it the end of any hope for recovery, there are the final lines of one of his last poems to consider. It's called "Phase Four" and refers to the final step of those in AA, which is surrendering to something or someone greater than oneself. It's the step that comes after Phase Three, which is the acceptance of who one is. But surrendering completely to the Father? Really? That seems to have been where Berryman—unlike Hopkins—finally balked. If "after finite struggle, infinite aid," he wrote, exhausted with it all, as he watched his one sane milkman recede across the bridge, if

ever you come there, friend,
remember backward me lost in defiance,
as I remember those admitting & complying.

We cannot tell the truth, it's not in us.
That truth comes hard. O I am fighting it,
my Weapon One. I know I cannot win,
and half the war is lost, that's to say won.

The rest is for the blessed. The rest is bells
at sundown off across a dozen lawns,
a lake, two strands of laurel, where they come
out of phase three mild toward the sacristy.

5
THE DUBLIN NOTEBOOK

I n the winter of 1885, the forty-year-old Hopkins brushed off a notebook he'd procured years earlier while a student at Oxford to use now for keeping notes and grading his students at University College, Dublin. It's a book that for Hopkins scholars has attained an almost mythic status thanks to what it tells us of Hopkins's life and state of mind during his time in Dublin. Now, at last, it has been made available to us all, thanks to Oxford University Press and the work of two first-rate scholars of Hopkins's work, Leslie Higgins and Michael Suarez, SJ, and it undoubtedly helps us better understand why this particular notebook is so important for understanding the man who gave us not only some of the most powerful poems written in his own generation, but—simply put—some of the most extraordinary poems ever composed.

For how else shall we describe poems like "To seem the stranger," "I wake and feel the fell of dark," "Carrion Comfort," "No worst, there is none," "Spelt from Sybil's Leaves," or Caradoc's havoc-ridden soliloquy from Hopkins's unfinished play, *St. Winifred's Well?* This last has Caradoc speaking to himself with the rest of us listening in just after he has beheaded the woman he is obsessed with because, turning the moral world perversely on its head, he needs her so much more deeply than he can fathom. It's a soliloquy that bears comparison with that of King Lear after the final loss of his daughter, or Milton's Satan as he prepares to spend forever in a hell of his own making, or Melville's Ahab, willing to take his entire crew down with him in his pursuit of a creature he has come to demonize for having taken his leg. Caradoc's speech, in fact, is the mask Hopkins employs as he meditates on the strange wonder he feels in realizing that he, too, can imagine striking back at the One who seems to have disappeared from his life.

Among the leaves of this notebook, we find drafts of both "Sybil's Leaves" and Caradoc's soliloquy mixed in with so much else that was on Hopkins's tortured mind then: leaves composed not so much of green grass yellowing, as with Whitman's leaves, as of the browned leaves of bitter spelt. Now at last it has come home to him that he is expendable, as he moves through the darkest months of his first year in a politically volatile Ireland that has already seen the assassination of two British leaders in Dublin's Phoenix Park.

To make matters worse, Hopkins now feels in his very marrow what it means to be at a "third remove" from his rare, dear England and Wales as well as his fellow English Jesuits. Too, he senses his increasing separation from close friends like Robert Bridges and Canon Richard Watson Dixon and Alexander William Mowbray Baillie. Then, too, there's his growing distance from his family as each member goes his or her own way, leaving behind the home he grew up in. All of this descends upon him now as the bleak winter darkness threatens to drown him in a relentless tide of depression and despair.

In the spring of 1884, Hopkins moved to 85–86 St. Stephen's Green, across from what was at the time the largest park in Europe, to settle in a room among the very buildings where the saintly Fr. John Henry Newman had come to start up a university for Irish Catholics at a time when being Catholic meant exclusion from Oxford, Cambridge, and

Trinity College, Dublin. It was here that Newman conceived of and wrote his magnificent *The Idea of a University*, modeled on his Oxford experience (or what he imagined Oxford to have been like prior to the changes imposed on the university by Henry VIII). But Ireland—struggling to rise again in the wake of the Irish potato famine of the 1840s, a catastrophe that had claimed a great number of Irish lives and caused many geographic displacements of families—was looking for a model different from what Newman imagined. And so, after a few years, Newman left Ireland and returned to England and his Birmingham Oratory, where the young Hopkins—himself, like Newman, a recent convert from Anglicanism—had taught when he was fresh out of Oxford and just before joining the Society of Jesus in Roehampton.

When Newman's idea of a university was resurrected by the Jesuits in 1883 as University College, Dublin (UC Dublin), the Irish Jesuit Fr. Delaney petitioned the English province for Jesuits who could teach classes as well as serve as examiners for those seeking entrance into one of Ireland's colleges. Such a university would facilitate an influx of Irish Catholics who had been denied a university education because of their faith. As hundreds upon hundreds of students sought admission to Ireland's colleges, the work of examining the applicants' ability to translate the classics and their knowledge of basic Greek and Roman history, literature, and grammar now fell in large part on Hopkins himself, the only Jesuit the English province could afford to send, and that because Hopkins was deemed an eccentric. Preparing and grading six national exams in Greek and Latin per year, in addition to teaching morning and evening classes, would have been daunting for anyone, but the burden fell on Hopkins's frail shoulders rather like a heavy wooden cross thudding down on his shoulders.

In addition to Hopkins's letters and poems written from Ireland, we have the beginnings of essays and notes on sermons and spiritual meditations for feast days and memorials, as well as scratched-out and revised translations from the Latin written in an idiomatic English.

We also have a copy of William Collins's eighteenth-century "Ode to Evening" that Hopkins jotted down from memory—which poem he would use as the scaffolding for his own "Sibyl's Leaves." And then there are his notes for a short biographical entry on his friend and fellow poet Canon Richard Watson Dixon, which Hopkins wrote for his University College Dublin colleague Thomas Arnold's *A Manual of English Literature, Historical and Critical,* published in 1885. There are also page after page of check marks, produced as Hopkins graded papers into the early insomniac hours of morning: those exam papers written in poor Latin and worse Greek because many of his students had not had adequate training in Caesar's *Gallic Wars* or Cicero's *On Duty* and possessed even less knowledge of the histories of Livy and Tacitus or the poetry of Catullus, Martial, and Juvenal.

Reading through the notebook can feel—to use a contemporary metaphor—rather like channel-surfing through Hopkins's mind, and there are many facets one could focus on. But what strikes me in particular is Hopkins's searching for a new music, one that would have its roots in Pindar's *Odes* and the Greek tragic choruses as well as in the development of plainchant. Such music, of course, predates the piano and the *sol fa* tradition by at least 2,500 years, and since Hopkins did not have an adequate notational system by which he could register that music on paper, the musicologists he consulted about it, like Sir Robert Stewart, thought Hopkins woefully ignorant of musical structures.

But what one hears in "Spelt from Sibyl's Leaves" and "That Nature is a Heraclitean Fire" is a music that strains to enflesh the human cry at the heart of Greek tragedy and Pindar's *Odes,* a music not so much for the piano as for something like the bagpipe, capable of recalling the bleat of a lost sheep or the desolate wail of suffering humanity—or perhaps even the cry of Christ from the cross, delivered as words failed him and all he could utter was a howl of desolation. For is that not what one is left with as one studies this broken-backed remnant of a notebook: the image of a despairing man who, like his Master, had started out with great promise and hope, and who could sense the finger of God in weeds and wilderness, in the winter stars and the flight of a windhover on a May morning in Wales, or in bluebells or the sound of a stone plunking into the bottom of a well, or the energy of a man plowing a muddy field, or in the innocent features of a young soldier—still more boy than man— who would soon be deployed to Afghanistan?

Important, too, for understanding Hopkins during this period are his meditation notes for his final eight-day retreat, which took place in early January 1889, at the Irish novitiate at St. Stanislaus's College in Tullabeg. The meditations described therein only reinforce Hopkins's feeling of desolation and his pervasive sense that everything he had done in serving the Irish youth in Dublin—at the same university that a young Irish Catholic named James Joyce would attend a decade after Hopkins was gone—had come at last to nothing.

Precisely here lies the paradox, of course, for out of his suffering and desolation, Hopkins created an equivalent to what Wilfred Owen, Isaac Rosenberg, and those other poets who served in the trenches of World War I produced from their own experiences. Or what Yeats belatedly articulated as a result of the *Troubles*. "Spelt from Sybil's Leaves" bears within it a music that we have become more accustomed to, a shuddering, complex, contrapuntal, psalmlike music, in which "selfwrung, selfstrung, sheathe- and shelterless, / thóughts agaínst thoughts ín groans grínd."[50] In-groan, ingrown—the words themselves speak of something pressing unrelentingly against the tortured mind.

In those final retreat notes, we find Hopkins reflecting on five wasted years as he endured a week of desolation in Tullabeg, days in which nothing came and he was left with only a dry, barren submission to the will of God. Then suddenly, in a flash, came a fall-gold wealth of insights into the mystery of Christ's life, and the exhausted Jesuit awoke to find that—as when, at the feast of Cana, Christ had turned six *amphorae* of water into wine of the first order—there had been no stint, only, perhaps, "an unwise order in the serving." Looking at human history from the perspective of two millennia removed, Hopkins asked himself: What matter the wars—or even the death—of Caesar (tiny stars now bleeding slivers of light), when his Master had quietly transformed everything? What matter those endless piles of papers on his desk in his cramped quarters? Was it not all in the long run just so much spelt? And cannot we, joining in Hopkins's reflection, say that what really matters is the impact he would have on the lives of those—then and now—he would come in contact with, in person and through his poems? Did he not, after all, turn even his suffering, both mental and spiritual, into a thing of extraordinary beauty for generations to come?

The *Dublin Notebook* is—how shall we say this?—indispensable in allowing us to see into the everyday workings of the poet's mind. There's the workaday world of grading exams, the poet-professor's thoughts on which classical authors to teach and to which classes: Caesar, Cicero, Sallust, Horace, Virgil, Homer, Sophocles, Thucydides, Euripides, Demosthenes, Plato, and Aristotle. And then there are his musings on music, comments on his friends' poetry, cursory thoughts on the largely unspoken pressures of the current political situation, the weather, and those brilliant momentary glimpses into both the spiritual barrenness and richness of the poet's mind.

All of this strikes us, fortunate as we are for these musings, like so many particles of grit and sand filtering through the mind of a poet of the first order. They invite us to glimpse something of his world, where often enough only his first, fast, last friend, Christ, seems present, if often only by his apparent absence. For all of us, but for the Christian poet especially, there is something of profound value here: those poems, those pearls of great price, which Hopkins and his Master have mercifully, thankfully, given us.

6
WHEN POETS WRITE LETTERS

A fter more than half a century, a new edition of the letters by and to Hopkins is finally available in two generous volumes. It's also the first time Hopkins's correspondence has been published in strictly chronological order, so that it is possible to get a sense of whom Hopkins was writing to and what others were writing back to him from the early 1860s, when he was living with his large family at Oak Hill, Hampstead, until his death. For decades we have waited for just such an edition. And what a resource we now have: everything arranged chronologically, along with some forty-three letters discovered since the earlier edition published back in 1956.

There are letters from William Addis, a friend who also converted to Catholicism and became a priest but, a year before Hopkins's death, left the priesthood and renounced his faith, to Hopkins's deep disappointment. Letters, too, to and from his fellow Jesuits Peter Gallwey, Francis Goldie, and Francis Bacon; from Alexander Mowbray Baillie; Edward Bond; Ernest Hartley Coleridge, the grandson of Samuel Taylor Coleridge; Richard Watson Dixon; Digby Dolben, Robert Bridges's handsome, wispy cousin, who drowned at nineteen, and to whom the young Hopkins felt a deep attraction; from William Garrett and Martin Geldart (who also drowned, and whom Hopkins was convinced had died a suicide); to and from John Henry Newman and Edward Pusey, the Tractarian who struggled to find a middle way between Roman Catholicism and Protestantism and worked alongside Newman until Newman converted; to and from the Irish poet Kate Tynan, part of the circle of the young William Butler Yeats; Coventry Patmore; Baron Francis de Paravicini of Balliol College, and his wife, Frances, who fondly remembered Hopkins after his death in a letter to his mother; William Urquhart; Alexander Wood; and Harry Wooldridge, who—at Bridges's suggestion—painted Hopkins's portrait in 1886 based on the black and white photograph taken of him at Oxford on the eve of his departure from there in 1879.

There's also the Hopkins clan: grandmother Ann; grandpapa John Simm Smith; aunts Annie and Katie; his parents, Manley and Kate; as well as his brothers, Cyril, Arthur, Lionel, and Everard; and his sisters Millicent, Kate, and Grace, most of whom lived on long after Gerard himself. Lionel, the longest living, died in his ninety-eighth year in 1952, at double his brother's age. And finally, there's Bridges himself, without whose mediation in preserving so many of his letters and poems Hopkins, except for the immediate circle of those whom he knew and served, would have entered the halls of oblivion long ago.

There are those letters that actually did enter that oblivion to ponder: the loss of letters Hopkins wrote and then discarded, because of some perceived scruple or dissatisfaction. "I could not get that letter finished," he wrote Bridges on July 23, 1877, "and have made up my mind not to go on with it."[51] And this at the very time he was composing his brilliant nature sonnets in the grace-filled months leading up to his ordination. Or the letter he began to Baillie in the late spring of 1880 while assigned to pastoral duties in the Irish working-class slums of Liverpool and, while sitting in the confessional box, took the occasion to confess that he'd decided to suppress what he'd written about the numbing conditions of working among the poor, the filthy, and the drunkards, work that was killing him, deciding to destroy the letter after reading what he'd written several times over, first with his head "on one side, then on the other."[52]

Five years later, during his short Easter holidays in April 1885, and exiled now to Dublin, he wrote Coventry Patmore that sometime back he'd written Patmore "a longish letter, but repented of it, as I often do, and did not send it."[53] And this at a time when he was undergoing that dark night of the soul that gave rise to many of his dark sonnets, including—most likely—"I wake and feel the fell of dark not day," "No worse, there is none," and "Carrion Comfort." In the letters themselves he admits to composing other letters, some of them lengthy, but then never sending them. Or beginning a letter and then using the paper on which the letter was begun to compose a few lines of poetry.

We know too that Bridges (who eventually became England's Poet Laureate) destroyed virtually every letter he ever wrote to Hopkins over a period of some twenty-four years. When those letters finally came back into his possession following Hopkins's death, he decided to burn them because he wanted no biography written about him, though many of his letters to others did survive and were subsequently published. But he thought Hopkins's letters too important to meet the same fate, and so he was careful to preserve them, though he did occasionally cut out names and sections of letters that he regarded as too personal, especially where Hopkins related something about his own family. We know—alas—that letters written to Hopkins as he lay dying were read and then destroyed by his mother as being of a private nature. And we also know that Hopkins destroyed a number of letters, especially from his family, as he went over his personal effects in his sparse quarters at 85 St. Stephen's Green in Dublin.

There's a list of every letter here, beginning with one written by his aunt or nurse from the Grove sometime in 1852, when Hopkins was seven or eight, followed by a tongue-in-cheek letter written in May of

1861, when Hopkins was sixteen, to a Dr. Müncke, a teacher of French and German at Highgate, where Hopkins was a student. It concerns an aesthetic and moral dilemma raised by Goethe in his *Faust* created when Mephistopheles would not offer Faust more of the higher pleasures and "subtle charms" afforded by poetry, music, and art. In this question alone we see the older Hopkins peeking through the young man.

The correspondence proliferates between 1866 and 1868, the years from Hopkins's conversion at the age of twenty-two to his entry into the Society of Jesus at twenty-four. Then the letters taper off as he undergoes his training as a novice at Manresa House in Roehampton outside London, then (as he continues the *Ratio Studiorum*) as a scholastic at St. Mary's, Stonyhurst, and finally as a theology student at St. Beuno's in North Wales. It is only after his ordination in September 1877 that the correspondence finally flourishes.

The major recipients of his letters in the last dozen years of his life are his closest friend, Robert Bridges, to whom he wrote most often and most openly, then his former teacher Richard Watson Dixon, and—beginning in August 1883, when he was teaching at Stonyhurst—the poet Coventry Patmore, who, try as he might, admitted that he never understood the poems Hopkins sent him. Then, too, there's Alexander Mowbray Baillie, his friend from his Oxford days, who became a London barrister, and who, though their paths did not often cross, reciprocated his deep sense of friendship in the letters they shared. In their 1886 exchange of letters (when Hopkins barraged Baillie with postcards about Egyptian cuneiform and the relationship of the Greek gods to the Egyptian gods and how that might be ascertained through their linguistic affinities), what most comes across is Hopkins's deep need in his loneliness to hear his old Oxford friend's honest and forthright voice once again.

For that is what one looks for and finds in these letters again and again: how important family and friends were to Hopkins: bonds formed while Hopkins was still living at home or at Oxford. These are deep friendships that became all the deeper as Hopkins grew older and began to understand at a far greater level the gift of friendship from his perspective as a Jesuit and as a priest. Then, too, there are his worries about the health of Bridges or Baillie or a member of his family, as he prays for them, wanting to be there for them to comfort them.

What's also evident in the letters is that wonderful sense of humor he had: the jokes, the awful Jesuit puns, the gentlemanly wit, the raucous, boisterous humor that he sometimes allows to escape. Here he is, in a letter to Bridges written in November 1887, remembering the drunken organist as Hopkins said Mass at St. Xavier's in Liverpool: "I have now twice had the experience," he writes. "It is distressing, alarming, agitating, but above all delicately comic; it brings together the bestial and the angelic elements in such a quaint entanglement as nothing else can; for 'musicians' never play such clever descants as under those circumstances and in an instant everybody is thrilled with the insight of the situation."[54]

Or the prank he pulled on an Irish friend who had tried to put one over on him, and whom he had warned he would return the favor. "Accordingly," he confessed to Bridges in October 1888, he'd written him a letter from

> the son of a respected livery and bait stables in Parteen sometimes employed by your Honoured Father 'asking for an introduction to one of the Dublin newspapers 'as reporter, occasional paregraphs [sic] or sporting intelligence.' The sentence I think best of was one in which I said I (or he) could 'give any color which may be desired to reports of speeches or Proceedings subject to the Interests of truth which must always be the paremount [sic] consideration.' It succeeded beyond my wildest hopes and action is going to be taken. The letter is even to be printed in the *Nation* as a warning to those who are continually applying in the like strain.[55]

To this Hopkins added, though, that he would have to step in and confess what he'd done as a practical joke by way of contributing to the current dictates of Irish political journalism.

In April 1889, Francis de Paravicini of Balliol was in Dublin and had spent an evening with Hopkins. When Paravicini returned home, he told his wife that Hopkins had looked "very ill" and seemed "much depressed," enough so that he and his wife had begged the English provincial to recall Hopkins back home, at least for a spell. Alas, it was too late, and Hopkins died on June 8. "He was so lovable," Paravicini's wife wrote Hopkins's mother six days later, "so singularly gifted—&, in his saintliness, so apart from, and so different to, all others. Only that his beautifully gentle and generous nature made him one with his friends; and led us to love & to value him—feeling that our lives were better, & the world richer, because of him."[56] How deeply those words must resonate for so many of Hopkins's readers, who can only know him now through his poems, his journals and notes, and these—his letters.

And what letters these are, striking us perhaps more forcibly in a culture that has largely neglected or lost altogether the treasure of this means of expression and communication. In an earlier age, though, the writing of letters was more than a discipline to be fulfilled. It was a means of discovery, an essential dimension of the poetic life. "This is my letter to the world," Emily Dickinson wrote,

> That never wrote to me,—
> The simple news that Nature told,
> With tender majesty.

What is it about poetry and letter-writing that the two should be so entwined? Is it because poetry is so personal, finally, with the "I" that writes to the Thou an expression of what we replicate when we actually take the time to write someone? Who is the poet's audience, finally? Whom do we address in our most intimate moments—a single self reaching out to another self, whether that self is a relative, a friend, a lover, a muse? Or is it some inner mirror of ourselves, finally, that we write to and for? We say the self, or oneself, or some aspect of the self by which we want to be recognized, and even appreciated. The utterer uttering to the one uttered, all recognized in the act of uttering.

A letter taped to the icebox by one's wife, as when Floss Williams, William Carlos Williams's wife, wrote, telling her husband what was in the icebox so he could make himself some lunch. The doctor-poet, so touched by that gesture of lovingkindness—one more such act by a loving wife—responded by writing a note to her in return in the form of a poem. This simple gesture, of course, was much more than a poem. It was a confession of who he really was and of his transgressive nature, asking her now for her forgiveness. "This is Just to Say," he wrote, condensing Milton's twelve books of *Paradise Lost* with its message of sinful pride and the crossing of boundaries into just twelve lines:

I have eaten
the plums
that were in
the icebox

and which
you were probably
saving
for breakfast

Forgive me
they were delicious
so sweet
and so cold

Letters, like poems, take all sorts of forms, and can tell us many things about ourselves, some funny, some serious, some banal, some profound. And more often than not, both reveal a good deal more than what we even thought we knew about ourselves.

7
WHAT THE WORLD CAN
TELL US

If Gerard Manley Hopkins the Jesuit priest wrote some of the great "Franciscan" poems of all time, he thus finds himself intimately bound to Pope Francis, a Jesuit who took the name of Francis, in several important ways. For one thing, it makes sense that Francis should begin *Laudato Si'*, his letter to the world fittingly delivered on Pentecost Sunday 2015, by quoting from St. Francis's "Canticle of the Creatures":

> Praise be to you, my Lord,
> through our Sister, Mother Earth,
> who sustains and governs us,
> and who produces various fruit
> with colored flowers and herbs.

Pope Francis begins his encyclical, subtitled *On Care for Our Common Home*, by citing his namesake, reminding us that "our common home is like a sister with whom we share our life and a beautiful mother who opens her arms to embrace us."[57] In the name of the Church, in the name of our shared humanity, he reminds us that the very earth "cries out to us because of the harm we have inflicted on her by our irresponsible use and abuse of the goods with which God has endowed her."

Hopkins, too, who loved God's Creation much as St. Francis did, wept over what humans were doing to the English and Welsh countryside and, by extension, to the entire world. One senses in his writings, as in the recent encyclical, a voice imploring, as if to say, "Forgive them, Father, for they know not what they do. You have showered them with love. You have given them this beautiful world, both on the cosmic as well as on the microcosmic level, if they only had ears to hear its music and eyes to see what is there before them, if they would only take the time to look."

But look at what? Hopkins's poems tell us what is there before us, just as Fr. Francis did before him and Pope Francis more recently. "Look at the stars!" Hopkins urges us in "The Starlight Night":

Look, look up at the skies!
O look at all the fire-folk sitting in the air!
The bright boroughs, the circle-citadels there!
Down in dim woods the diamond delves! the elves'-eyes!
The grey lawns cold where gold, where quick gold lies!
Wind-beat white beam! airy abeles set on a flare!
Flake-doves sent floating forth at a farmyard scare!

This is Van Gogh's *Starry Night* in a language rinsed and refreshed, words with a sense of deep wonder and awe behind them. Do you hear it? Can you see it? Get up from your chair and go out behind your house on a clear dark night where you can actually see the stars, and let their immensity and beauty surround you, he tells us. It's all free and there for the taking, he urges us on with nine exclamations in seven lines.

Ah, the stars: stars as fire-folk, as bright boroughs, as circle-citadels. Or, in a reversal, diamond delves, elves' eyes, quicksilver gold: stars like the white underside of poplars shining in the night sky. All that energy and life, like a flock of spooked doves suddenly lifting from the earth, and behind those millions of dancing stars, behind those millions of gold pieces, is something even greater: the Creator of it all, the Father and "Christ and his mother and all his hallows." A taste of heaven there for the asking.

"The world is charged with the grandeur of God," Hopkins wrote that same month. And if the world is charged with that grandeur, then we are charged with acknowledging it, since we are the only creatures consciously aware of that beauty and so of praising the Creator of Brother Sun and Sister Moon, and, in a startling side glance—which just may bear repeating—those "grey lawns cold where gold, where quick gold lies." For who else is to witness to the terrible effects of strip-mining that leave huge brow-like slags to scar the earth for generations after? How else can the earth cry out in its hurt? What other "eye, tongue, or heart else, where / Else, but in dear and dogged man?" Man, so dear to his Creator, and yet so self-bent on himself that he would strip "our rich round world bare," without a care for those who come after. Methane in the air we breathe, lead in the water we drink, waste everywhere.

And the poor, the poor everywhere, their dignity stripped from them. "Undenizened, beyond bound / Of earth's glory, earth's ease," he wrote late in his too-short life.[58] The unemployed no longer a viable part of the commonwealth, and no one to share that care: this, he warned us, was to weigh those about us down with a hangdog dullness, a dullness that would morph to despair and then rage, turning those hangdogs to manwolves, whose packs would infest the age. *Laudato si'*, please God. *Laudato si'*.

Praise: isn't this a vital dimension of the poets' task, a dimension of our responsibility, one central to the poet's vocation, really? Praise as bearing witness to the radiant beauty that is God's gift to us? Isn't it our task to sing of that beauty to be found even in the meanest things—the way for example Hopkins would study the supple veins and variegations of color in a single oak leaf, or Williams would pick up a pulp of maple leaves off the sidewalk and breathe in their exquisite, life-refreshing scent? Or John Berryman, signaling the first inklings of spring, writing:

—It is Spring's New England. Pussy willows wedge
up in the wet. Milky crestings, fringed
yellow, in heaven, eyed
by the melting hand-in-hand. . . .

Or Hart Crane, gazing across the East River toward lower Manhattan, between the Brooklyn Bridge to his right and the Statue of Liberty to his left ninety years ago, the image as fresh now as when he wrote it:

How many dawns, chill from his rippling rest
The seagull's wings shall dip and pivot him,
Shedding white rings of tumult, building high
Over the chained bay waters Liberty. . . .

And so it goes, this news, as the young Ezra Pound once wrote, poetry—"news that stays news."

Add to all this the Good News, which stays and sustains the Catholic poet, with the image of the crucified Christ, God's only Son, before us, the good news that somehow, *somehow*, in spite of the damage we go on creating, the Creator too goes on creating, fixing and mending as only the Creator can, because, as Hopkins wrote, the good Lord, fathering and mothering us, sadly and magnificently, goes on . . . and on. Why all of this, if not because of the instress of truth that invites us to see that here and now, in our midst,

There lives the dearest freshness deep down things;
And though the last lights off the black West went
Oh, morning, at the brown brink eastward, springs —
Because the Holy Ghost over the bent
World broods with warm breast and with ah! bright wings.

II
IN ORDINARY TIME

VARIATIONS ON A THEME
IN MODERN AMERICAN POETRY

8
WALLACE STEVENS,
MYSTERY MAN

T hinking about Wallace Stevens, one keeps coming back to what appears to be the irresolvable double nature of a man who spent much of his life as a busy insurance company lawyer and at the same time became an American poet standing alongside Whitman and Dickinson, and perhaps above Eliot, Williams, Berryman, and Bishop. Try to sum him up by way of biography and here is what you might come up with.[59] Born on October 2, 1879, in Reading, Pennsylvania, the second of five children of Pennsylvania Dutch parents, Wallace Stevens claims an American ancestry going back to when New York was still New Amsterdam. His father was a successful lawyer who in midlife suffered devastating financial reversals followed by a nervous breakdown. He grew up in Reading until he left for Harvard, which he attended from 1897 to 1900 in a three-year accelerated program (to save his father, who had three sons in college, some money), and then went down to Manhattan to try his hand at newspaper reporting. Within a year, however, he left journalism and entered law school. Then, after a failed attempt at private practice with a former Harvard classmate, he moved over to the insurance business, in large part because he was more at ease working with complicated legal documents than he was with human beings.

He read incessantly—the classics in literature and philosophy, including Plato's *Dialogues*, Aristotle, Longinus, Dante, Shakespeare, Milton, Wordsworth, Keats, and especially Coleridge. He also read philosophy: Kant, Schopenhauer, and Nietzsche, together with Henry James and Robert Louis Stevenson as well as the French and German literary classics—in the original—which is how he first encountered the philosophical notebooks of Simone Weil in the early 1940s. Among his Harvard professors with whom he felt a close connection was his mentor and model, a Spanish agnostic who defined himself as an aesthetic Catholic: George Santayana, poet and philosopher.

Stevens would live and work in New York City from 1900 to 1916. In 1909, he married Elsie Kachel, his dream girl, also from Reading, who clerked and played piano in a sheet music store. His parents found her below family standards and refused to attend the wedding, which took place just three blocks from where Stevens had grown up. Wallace and Elsie remained faithful to their vows, but their marriage itself soured quickly, so that Stevens soon found himself relegated to a solitary, if plush, attic bedroom, where for consolation he listened to Jack Benny and opera on the radio. Early on, he wrote poems, especially sonnets, which he gathered in two collections for Elsie on her birthday in 1907 and 1908. But he did not begin publishing his poetry until 1914, when he was thirty-five. Then, within a three-year period, he published in journals and magazines many of the poems by which he is still best known, including "Sunday Morning," "The Snow Man," and "The Emperor of Ice-Cream."

In 1916, he and Elsie moved to Hartford, Connecticut, the insurance capital of America, where Stevens went to work at the Hartford Accident and Indemnity Insurance Company. Each morning and evening he walked the two miles between his home and his grand office in the Hartford building, composing his poems during those daily perambulations. His first book, *Harmonium*, appeared in 1923 and was well received by several critics, if not by the public. He would go on to publish seven more volumes during his lifetime, earning a Bollingen Prize (1949), two National Book Awards (1951 and 1955), and, for his 1954 *Collected Poems*, a Pulitzer. He and Elsie had one child, a daughter, Holly, born when Stevens was in his mid-forties.

An able and diligent lawyer, Stevens was named a vice president at the Hartford in 1934. He was not known there—or in most other places—for warmth and sensitivity. Once, a colleague told Stevens that he'd admired a eulogy Stevens had given at the funeral of another Hartford executive, to which Stevens replied, "I hope to do the same for you some day." In 1955, the same colleague, on learning that Stevens had died, asked if it was a heart attack, noting that he would be surprised to learn that Stevens ever had a heart.[60]

Stevens was a large man—six feet two, 240 pounds—and in photos seems to tower over whoever stood near him. Not suited for leadership or working closely with others, he met with other lawyers and courthouse officials only when necessary. For his last decades on the job, he worked in large part by dictating memoranda and letters to his secretaries, who were also largely responsible for the typescripts of his poems over the years.

His literary relationships were no warmer. He tried to goad Robert Frost into an exchange of insults, but Frost demurred. Each February for twenty years Stevens spent several weeks in the Florida Keys, mostly Key West. He was known to drink, and he could be unruly when he drank too much. On one well-known occasion he provoked a fistfight with Ernest Hemingway, twenty years his junior, that left Stevens with a bruised, swollen face and a hand he broke on Hemingway's jaw.

For reasons that may have to do with his witnessing the collapse of his father's business, Stevens stayed with the Hartford after he became an honored literary figure, working there even after he was diagnosed at seventy-five with the cancer that killed him. Months before his death, he turned down a prestigious lectureship at Harvard because he was afraid that his absence for an academic year would cost him his job. He died an employee of the Hartford.

He worked hard there, eventually becoming known as the King of Surety (a method of contract protection). Still, he managed to find the time necessary to compose hundreds upon hundreds of exquisite poems, usually on those walks between home and work. Reaching the Hartford in the morning, he would hand his secretaries, for typing, the lines he'd written in a scrawl only they could understand. It is no mistake that you can feel the steady iambic beat of those lines grounded in the repetition of the one-two steps he repeated each day.

In spite of this, Stevens was a stunning and original poet, a Modernist and a Romantic, as well as a visionary in quest of what he called in "The Necessary Angel" "the supreme truth," or—alternatively—"the real." Here was someone pursuing a language and a music capable of nourishing, delighting, and comforting both the writer and his readers in the face of whatever social, political, and economic troubles humans of his time were compelled to endure, including—thanks to Marx, Nietzsche, Freud, and a host of others—the eclipse of God.

By the time Stevens turned thirty-five, he believed he had found the music he had been searching for. First came a form of poetry that captured something of the New York avant-garde, as original in its own way as the paintings of Picasso, Matisse, and Duchamp that had stunned viewers in the 1913 New York Armory Show. These are the poems, collected in *Harmonium*, that most people think of when they recall Stevens, like "Thirteen Ways of Looking at a Blackbird," whose haiku-like sections summon, with chiseled courage, the end that awaits all:

> It was evening all afternoon.
> It was snowing
> And it was going to snow.
> The blackbird sat
> In the cedar-limbs.

In his signature poem, "Sunday Morning," also from that early collection, Stevens addresses a modern young woman who lounges with coffee and oranges in her New York City apartment on an Easter Sunday, assuring her that she's made the right choice in staying home, for "The tomb in Palestine / Is not the porch of spirits lingering. / It is the grave of Jesus, where he lay." But that pronouncement could not, finally, satisfy Stevens, for he spent the rest of his life searching for the "real"—the extraordinary—hidden within the ordinary. His later poems, which are not as widely known as his earlier work, keep returning to and revising his earlier assertions.

Between the publication of *Harmonium* in 1923 and 1932, Stevens stopped writing poetry altogether. He felt he'd written himself into a corner and needed a new poetics and a new poetry if he was to speak to a radically changing time. By the mid-1930s, those new realities included the American Depression and long bread lines and an unemployment rate that exceeded 25 percent of the workforce. There was also the rise of international Communism, as well as the specter of Mussolini's and Franco's Fascism, Nazism, and Japanese imperialism. Stevens was in his early fifties when he returned to poetry, but when he came back, it was with a force that sustained him until his death in 1955.

The path to recovery was not easy. He tried responding to the issues of the day, including the Spanish Civil War and Mussolini's incursions into Abyssinia. But before long he understood that these were not his subjects. His was the search for what underlay such events—that is, the problem of evil, and what he called the "real." To do this, he needed a language capable of taking on that theme, a poetics steeped simultaneously in both the quotidian and the deepest philosophical abstractions. Consider "The Men That Are Falling" (1936),[61] written as it became clear that the Spanish Loyalists were losing their struggle against Franco, Mussolini, and Hitler. Here the poet lies in his bed in Hartford at midnight, unable to sleep. Then, as he stares at his pillow, it morphs into a *sudarium*, the traditional Jewish cloth placed over the head of someone crucified. This, then, is the Christlike man willing to die for a cause he ardently believes in:

What is it he desires?

But this he cannot know, the man that thinks,
Yet life itself, the fulfillment of desire

In the grinding ric-rac, staring steadily
At a head upon the pillow in the dark . . .

Thick-lipped from riot and rebellious cries,

The head of one of the men that are falling, placed
Upon the pillow to repose and speak,

Speak and say the immaculate syllables
That he spoke only by doing what he did. . . .

This death was his belief though death is a stone.
This man loved earth, not heaven, enough to die.[62]

In the end, Stevens's quest became a search for the foundational sacredness of the everyday: the bird, the plum, the vase of roses, the chair in his room, or the ordinariness, commemorated in a 1950 poem, of an evening spent in New Haven. "It is a kind of total grandeur at the end," he wrote toward the close of this long poem titled "To an Old Philosopher in Rome," a reflection on his mentor George Santayana, himself dying in a convent in Rome and cared for by nuns in blue habits:

With every visible thing enlarged and yet
No more than a bed, a chair, and moving nuns,
The immense theatre, the pillared porch,
The book and candle in your ambered room,

Total grandeur of a total edifice,
Chosen by the inquisitor of structures
For himself. He steps upon this threshold,
As if the design of all his words takes form
And frame from thinking and is realized.

I have read and taught Stevens now for over fifty years. He is someone who never ceases to delight. Admittedly, he is difficult, but meditating on his poems is worth the effort. And though he speaks to many different sensibilities, including atheism and agnosticism, it surprises and comforts me how synchronous his poems are with the Catholic sensibility of things—namely, the sense in which God's imagination and the human imagination, if we are fortunate, mesh and fuse.

As he wrote in what turned out to be his final poem, "Of Mere Being,"[63] "You know then that it is not the reason / That makes us happy or unhappy." In the end it will be a "gold-feathered bird" singing in the palms a song "without human meaning, / Without human feeling, a foreign song." What will greet us will not be a flawed reality, but something far greater than ourselves, something to comfort and surprise—a vision where, like the emblazoned Spirit, "The bird's fire-fangled feathers dangle down."

9
THE AURORAS OF AUTUMN

Nineteen forty-seven. Wallace Stevens at sixty-eight, finishing up a distinguished career as both Hartford insurance executive and celebrated poet, composes what has come to be, perhaps, his capstone poem.[64] After a lifetime of trying to understand both what life is and what poetry can tell us about that life, he has arrived at this point: the solitary figure looking up at the grand spectacle of the Northern Lights, by which any of us must feel both awed and dwarfed to insignificance. Crispin-Stevens, the comedian as the letter *c* revisited once again, and once again, though even more starkly, the perceiving mind confronts and is overwhelmed by what it sees: the thing itself: Fate, Ananke, the serpent of Time shedding its skin yet again. Here we come full force to confront the sublime majesty and terror of it all, washing away every color but the bleak blackness and bleached white of the vanishing, insistent Omega.

This, yes, and a sense of that other terrible Sublime, this one created by our own species and then unleashed on it: the Bomb, that ultimate light and sound spectacle, a cloud expanding like a flower, with a light like ten thousand suns, annihilating every last human who stops and turns upon the sand to stare into its terrible still-forming face.

What all this points to is the end of innocence, that is, if ever there was a time and place for innocence except in the hungering mind. The deserted cabin on the beach—one more empty house among Stevens's houses, whether his family's home growing up in Reading, long since as with his parents and siblings now gone. Or his empty house in Hartford, filled with so many regrets and silences. And the mother, who made their house a home, gone now, long gone, all but the memories of her singing to the accompaniment of an accordion, as Stevens self-protectively mocks even that memory before letting it go as irretrievable, an irritant to get rid of so that, unencumbered, he may face the polar north and the serpentlike Aurora Borealis.

Ditto the lost father, the God-figure, the patriarch, fetching "negresses" to dance among the children in some madcap mock antebellum scene out of *Gone with the Wind*, with Atlanta in the background burning. What are we after all, he wonders, but figures in a masque, a play? Except that "there is no play," for we are people acting out improvised scripts "merely by being here." No progression, then, no denouement, no trombone crescendo ending or lone, lingering cello note drifting into the silences.

No, the play is elsewhere, and not with us, as Stevens senses. Like Hopkins sixty years before, overwhelmed by the clouds performing above him on a July day in Dublin—"Cloud puffball, torn tufts, tossed pillows" flaunting "forth on an airbuilt thoroughfare," which becomes a playful giant wrestling and tossing the earth itself bare, and us with it—so, too, Stevens realizes that it is the clouds that make up the true theater, the ultimate reality show:

A theatre floating through the clouds,
Itself a cloud, although of misted rock
And mountains running like water, wave on wave.
Through waves of light.

Waves of light, like the cold light of the Aurora Borealis. Like the light (and heat) of the Bomb. As in an abstract-expressionist painting, say, by Jackson Pollock. A force field, an energy, a cosmic serpent shedding its skins again and again, the world gone over to formlessness, except in the propensity of the imagination to make form out of formlessness. And, for Stevens, all this points to an energy force field he has witnessed spreading across the northern reaches of our planet, a serpent, at once terrifying and yet in itself innocent of any design on the miniscule beholder who beholds the ever-changing shapeless shape there in the arctic dark.

But can the imagination contain such a force, the thing we name that remains, after all—like Yahweh—nameless? Can we ever tame it? Or tame even our own mocking, reverent, questioning, relentless minds? We presume that our little houses will protect us, or so we like to think, but these—like our very bodies—may seem fortresslike for a time, but are helpless against Necessity's rifle-butt knock on the door:

> He opens the door of his house

> On flames. The scholar of one candle sees
> An Arctic effulgence flaring on the frame
> Of everything he is. And he feels afraid.

Here we come once again upon the *IS*: "I am all at once what Christ is," Hopkins ends his Heraclitean cloud-flux poem with a Johannine affirmation of *IS*, God's own signature, "because he was what I am." But Stevens is far more tentative and unsure and finally terrified by the thought of the imminent obliteration of all he is and knows. Only the imagination is real, William Carlos Williams insisted, and Stevens concurs, so that while everything will be reduced to whatever ash the world's wildfire leaves behind—some "shivering residue, chilled and foregone"—still, what remains is the imagination's "crown and mystical cabala."

Yet even the imagination has its limits. The curse of an insistent self-consciousness, for one, so that even the imagination "dare not leap by chance in its own dark." For to do so would be suddenly to metamorphose from one's grand "destiny to slight caprice," the whole divine turned on its head by a clap of the hands or some irreverent punch line:

And thus its jetted tragedy, its stele
And shape and mournful making move to find
What must unmake it and, at last, what can,
Say, a flippant communication under the moon.

And yet, Stevens's ten cantos tell us by degrees, there surely may be a time of innocence. Or at least the idea of a time and a place where innocence played once, or what's a childhood for? Once upon a time, this Hamletizing Hamlet laments,

We were Danes in Denmark all day long
And knew each other well, hale-hearted landsmen,
For whom the outlandish was another day
Of the week, queerer than Sunday.

In that world whose other name was Reading, in that world of sixty years before,

We thought alike
And that made brothers of us in a home
In which we fed on being brothers, fed
And fattened as on a decorous honeycomb.

But that was then. Now the house that was a home is no more, and the brothers (and sisters) are gone. As we grow older, like Stevens, we realize we have dreamed our lives away, stuck in the honey of sleep, aware more and more now of a world in which only two are real: the poet and his one faithful companion, the Muse, mother of his poems. But how sure can he be even of her? Or, for that matter, even of himself? Winter is coming on once more, he knows, for he can see Orion putting on his glittering belt in the long nights of late autumn. Still, it might come, some final, comforting rendezvous, in this, Stevens's version of Becket's *Waiting for Godot*. It might. It might. It just might come. Tomorrow, say, tomorrow,

> . . . in the simplest word,
> Almost as part of innocence, almost,
> Almost as the tenderest and the truest part.

What Stevens knows, finally, is that the auroras in and of themselves have no more design on us mortals than Shelley's Mont Blanc had on the poet, or even that terrible iceberg that married the Titanic in Hardy's "The Convergence of the Twain." Ice and snow and polar lights mean us no harm, because they do not mean. It is we, Stevens realizes, who must make our necessary adjustments, "Contriving balance to contrive a whole," as if Emerson's Poet had to undergo a radical new stock-taking of his central position as all-seeing eye, taking in "The full of fortune and the full of fate / As if he lived all lives."

What is there to see, he wonders with us, other than the wind shaking one's house here in his "hall harridan," where wind "haggles with weather and weather with wind"? For it is by such lights—the light of the imagination and the serpentine flickering of the cosmos—that one comes to experience the momentary "blaze of summer straw, in winter's nick."[65]

If Santayana was, as he defined himself, an "aesthetic Catholic," being cared for by those blue nuns at the end in the Eternal City, that is not where Stevens concluded his own journey. In his seventies, Stevens quipped, he had come to believe that he had to make up his mind about God, before God made up His mind about Stevens. And because I have taught and read and researched Stevens now for as long or longer than Stevens did the same for Santayana, it is comforting to me—as it is

THE AURORAS OF AUTUMN   153

to other Catholic writers—that Stevens should have moved inexorably from the real to the Real. At the end, as he lay dying in St. Francis Hospital a few streets over from his home on the western edge of Hartford, according to the hospital chaplain, Fr. Hanley, Stevens took the sacraments and came into the Church. The later poetry, of course, as in his elegy for Santayana himself, "To an Old Philosopher in Rome," would already seem to point to this. "It is as if in a human dignity," he wrote there, "Two parallels become one, a perspective, of which / Men are part both in the inch and in the mile." What he imagined Santayana seeing at the end remains unclear, as such mysteries must, where for us "The extreme of the known" must remain "in the presence of the extreme / Of the unknown," for the dying, a shape perceived within a confusion among the "bed and books," the light of the candle

>   tearing against the wick
>   To join a hovering excellence, to escape
>   From fire and be part only of that which
>   Fire is the symbol: the celestial possible.

He is such an incredible poet, this Stevens, one who continues to comfort and haunt me sixty years on, and who speaks to me as for others—if the truth be told—again and again and again. Here he is: the poet searcher for whom Matisse's chapel of light there in southern France—a sacred place Stevens never visited but which he evoked again and again—became a metaphor for that "total grandeur of a total edifice," a refuge chosen by the poet, that "inquisitor of structures" in his search for a total edifice for himself and, yes, for real presence. And now, now that he has found it, not simply for himself as a person, but as a witness, too, for so many of us,

>   He stops upon this threshold,
>   As if the design of all his words takes form
>   And frame from thinking and is realized.

10
THE RIVER OF LANGUAGE

The language, the river of language washing constantly over us, even in our sleep: in sensing this William Carlos Williams was no different from any young poet starting out who must try on any number of voices in order to discover those he could call his own.[66] He, too, ransacked the various anthologies of poets, settling on Keats among the English Romantics and Whitman among his American predecessors. And so he imitated them, turning out bad Keats and bad Whitman both: the doe-eyed lyric and the ersatz demotic. He learned what he could from his college friend Ezra Pound, two years his junior, who would soon shake the dust of America from his feet and sail for Venice and then London, to sit at the feet of Yeats, and insisting that Bull Williams back there in Rutherford, New Jersey, do the same. In addition, he scolded Williams into reading Browning and the ballads and the prose of Henry James, as later he would champion Joyce and Eliot along with Wyndham Lewis and Ford Madox Ford. Here was the living vortex of language, to be found in Europe or among the work of Horace and Virgil or the author of *The Seafarer* or the medieval troubadours or Guido

Cavalcanti or the Elizabethan lyricists who instinctively understood the meaning of *melopoeia*. And, further afield, one hears echoes of the ancient poetry of Japan and Cathay.

But those were still-living forces residing elsewhere and in other times, and except for a year studying medicine in Leipzig and a visit to Rome to see his brother and another to London to meet up with Pound and a European sabbatical at forty, Williams remained in Paterson in northern New Jersey and New York, interning at the old French Hospital and then Children's Hospital further uptown, before setting up an office in his parents' house in Rutherford. But New York too, in the years leading up to the Great War, like Chicago, was bristling with the arts and manifestoes and little magazines being printed in studios and sheds. There were the Manhattan salons, of course, and the art galleries, like the one run by the photographer Alfred Stieglitz and Georgia O'Keefe. And there was the 1913 Armory Show, with its Cézannes and Matisses and Braques and Picassos, as well as the darker pigments of those New York tenement scenes and bars like McSorley's and Ashcan back alleys, or those sweating boxers pummeling one another in the dense cigar smoke enveloping the spectral, leering onlookers.

And there was a new generation of American poets already searching, like Walt Whitman of Brooklyn before them, for what they took to be a distinctive American language: Robert Frost up in Massachusetts and New Hampshire, or Carl Sandburg and Vachel Lindsay out in Chicago, or the rhythm-and-blues-haunted Langston Hughes up in Harlem, or the Harvard poets like E. E. Cummings and Wallace Stevens. Or the bohemian voices of Maxwell Bodenheim and Alfred Kreymborg and Lola Ridge and Mina Loy, voices pulled under by the vast, impersonal currents of time.

Consider other revolutions of the time: the skyscraper and the new verticality as opposed to gewgaw Victoriana, the Ford flivver and the Detroit assembly lines that made that phenomenon possible, as well as canneries and assembly lines of every sort, from the East Coast to the West. Consider, too, the new journalism and the typographical revolutions and the portable typewriter with its return tab and lower-case words at the beginning of each line. Or, more massively, the Great War and the Russian Revolution, bringing with them a new darkness as well as new possibilities, including for young Williams a sense that the old forms—the blank-verse line, the sonnet, the sestina, the villanelle, rhymed verse—ought to be replaced now with a sense of how the line might be formed and reformed, broken or extended or drastically reduced. Hadn't Gertrude Stein blown apart traditional syntax in the same way that Braque and Picasso had blown apart the image, turning them into shards of intersecting color and design, or Georges Antheil with his new music (replete with whirring propellers) had managed to shatter music, in much the same way that our buzzing thoughts crossed and crisscrossed one another constantly, and without end? *Per omnia saecula saeculorum.*

And what of Joyce's *Ulysses*, which managed to catalog (and parody) every aspect of the English language from its Anglo-Saxon roots through Chaucer and Shakespeare and Milton and Pope and all the way through to the skritching riffs of New World jazz and the street-slang of a living, breathing Anglo-Irish idiom in a way analogous to what St. Thomas Aquinas had with a jovial hullabaloo minutely examined the myriad layers of the language itself?

Break it, then, Williams came to understand, and practice, by the time he was thirty. Break the language and begin again, and then begin again and again, in spite of Stevens warning him against doing so, urging him to settle for a finished style instead—Cézanne, he might have said, rather than Juan Gris or Picasso. But what Williams wanted was to get back to the first forms of words and things, the language rinsed of its accumulated carbuncles of meaning, to see the thing itself, like Matisse intent on using a palette of primary colors only. Call it a river, then, the river of language, a living currency—yes, an imagined source of energy, but a living, vital currency of new coinage, too, and one of inestimable value: the language everywhere about him, with its complex rhythms, its sentences left unfinished because what had to be said had been said, and understood, before the sentence rounded on. . . . Words dancing with their one-two iambic patterns, or breaking against that, like a limping dog or an engorged satyr hobbling merrily along. Words counterpointed, contrapuntal, clashing against each other like atomic particles or drips and smatterings of far-flung paint, as in one of Jackson Pollack's Action paintings, the white canvas become one mass of energy mimicking the imagination of the artist, the empty field become a mix of randomness and design dancing together. Paint itself. Words themselves. An energy force field released as light, charged uranium particles enlightening us, surprising us, the charged, heady, and erotic delight of the goddess revealed, and the poet helping us to see there the thing itself, the actual rose in the ceramic urinal (thank you, Marcel): the thing reimagined and reassembled, refreshed and rinsed and renewed, glazed now with a finish of rainwater, upon which of course so much depended.

Make it of this, then: of this and this and this, Williams insisted. Behold the world itself right there before one, here, now, in Paterson—the filthiest swill hole in all of America, as Williams himself once described it, but refreshed and fed by the waters of the Passaic, just as the Arno fed Florence or the Seine Paris or the Thames London. True, the rivers had been degraded now by generations intent largely on buying and selling, just as the old myths of Greece and Rome had been degraded, though still—yes—capable of their original and elemental power and force and energy, like the Great Falls at Paterson with the currents running through and on further down through Rutherford, where he'd been born and would practice medicine and deliver thousands of babies and eventually die eighty years on, while the river flowed on downstream through Newark—a city as inaptly named as New Haven—to merge forever with the flintbacked Atlantic.

It is this, then, that one comes to understand the hunger for a living language to satisfy the imagination, a language shaped first by the

particulars of time and history and place, and then—again—by the poet
who listens. It is this language that has appealed to so many American
poets over the past hundred years. Hart Crane caught something of it
in various sections of his epic, *The Bridge,* as did the young Yvor Winters,
early drawn to—as later he would be repelled by—what Williams
insisted he had found. Stevens, too, who was of three minds about
"Wild Bill," that Carlos of the evanescent firefly candles, winking and
twinkling. And H. D., too, who scolded Williams for spitting on the
classic beauties he had wrought, only to abandon them in despair. And
Marianne Moore, whom Williams saw as a brilliant sister in the search
for a new way of saying. And of course his friend Ezra.

And then there were the younger poets, those who had schooled
themselves first at the feet of Eliot and his American disciple Allen
Tate, who then crossed over to Williams's side of the language divide
sometime in the 1950s: Kenneth Rexroth and Theodore Roethke,
along with Lowell and Berryman and Randal Jarrell. And, within a few
years, the river exponentially widened and deepened to include Allen
Ginsberg and Charles Olson and Robert Creeley and Denise Levertov,
as well as Paul Blackburn and Frank O'Hara and Amiri Baraka and Philip
Levine and W. S. Merwin, along with Charles Tomlinson and David
Ignatow and Cid Corman and Kenneth Koch and Joel Oppenheimer,
and of course James Laughlin, Williams's publisher from the 1930s on.

Beyond these, other poets, too, read Williams and found something
there that resonated deeply with them, even when, as often happens,
what they understood seems a misprision of the man. Still, something
there struck deeply, as in the hollow of a bell, with Marvin Bell and Bill
Heyen and Wendell Berry and Robert Bly and Charles Bernstein and
Stephen Dunn and Clarence Major and Ed Hirsch.

The clipped, jagged line, the long line reminiscent of Whitman
and Ford Madox Ford, the triadic step-down line, the variable foot,
the subtle or jigging internal chiming keeping the ear deliciously off
balance. And the living, breathing images of sycamores and locust trees,

of meadow cattails and strewn petals along the falls, a man in an old army coat warming himself on a stoop in Paterson, a woman eating a plum or standing on one foot while peering into the cheap shoe for the tiny nail that has been bothering her, a girl walking down the street, quickly looking down at her own jiggling breasts hidden beneath her new sweater, a cat negotiating several pots on a shelf, one foot then the next, a fire engine racing down a New York City street, its sirens sounding and its bells clanging, then disappearing in the muffling gray of a cold, steady rain. Call it the Zen tactility, *pace* Kant, of *das Ding an sich*, "the thing itself." Call it one of Hopkins's inscapes observed and presented in words, minus only its anagogical component.

Say it, then: no ideas but in things. Some probe Dr. Williams for the way he managed to dissect and observe the living language, deconstructed, reconstructed, sounds puzzling and even mysterious in all their shimmering self-containment, a light emanating from the womblike alembic of the imagination separating out of the darkness, the poet's uncanny and refreshing ability to present a century's centuries-old scene as if no time had passed between the then and the now, as if painted only this morning.

Still other poets wonder if anyone is really listening, if people ever take the time to actually see what is there before them, or can hear the music of the language about them, the thing itself lifted from the filthy river of desecrated time and rinsed clean and shining again as on the eighth day of creation. Persephone, Kora in hell, returning from the murkiness about us into the light again, if only for a moment, before she is pulled back under by the constant distractions of what passes for the quotidian, so that we die every day, again and again and again, for lack of the news, the real news, that only the poem can give us.

Make it of this, then, of this and this and this, poet, wherever you find yourself—in all senses of that phrase—like a lone star shining in the brilliant sunrise, toward which you add no part. So Williams, in his deep modesty and despair, believed, or seemed to believe, though something in him surely knew better. For he also understood that he was old rocky face, persisting even as the falls of the river rolled over like language itself, whether heard on the radio or television or read each day in the newspapers and the weeklies or—in our time—the blog-saturated word and the iPad, Facebook, and Skype and whatever else is out there waiting to distract us. In spite of which he listened and taught us to listen for the dance of the syllables, the design of those authentic notes that somehow prevail against the insistent chatter that would drown us if it could—a sense of presence to which we are called to be present, which Stevens knew as "the real," and Williams as the "thing itself."

11
"NOT LESS THAN EVERYTHING"

On the morning of January 7, 1972, at the close of the third year of the presidency of Richard Milhous Nixon, with the Jabberwock's war to end all wars still mired in those mind-numbing fetid marshes, Professor John Berryman, once showered with Pulitzers and other signs of recognition for his brilliant, game-changing poems, bearded and stoop-shouldered scholar (a.k.a. Henry) trudged across the campus of the University of Minnesota in gelid Minneapolis before halting on the cement pedestrian walkway that crosses the upper Mississippi at that point.

From this vertiginous vantage, the mighty Mississippi looks dwarfish, and there's a malebolge-like coal strip sidling up to its banks a hundred feet below. It was here that Professor Berryman, as his hero Hart Crane had balanced on the stern rail of the *SS Orizaba* forty years earlier, likewise balanced on a high metal rail as students rushed to classes that morning. Like Crane before him, he waved to those around him, then plunged through the unforgiving air. He was fifty-seven, had been in AA and dry for the past eleven months, before he courted a bottle of whiskey and downed a few too many.

Two days earlier he'd scribbled out one last poem, fittingly a Dream Song with a missing final line, in which he explained how he meant to escape what he saw now was in the cards—that the lectures he'd prided himself on were sure to fall short of his own expectations, and that would mean students

> dropping the course,
the Administration hearing
& offering me either a medical leave of absence
Or resignation. . . .

Well, he had a better plan for keeping the cops and his wife and everyone else off his back. All it took to make a man would be a simple tilt forward, sans knife blade to the throat, and then the struggle would be over.

So how is it that this apostate, this renegade, this brilliant American poet who had lived through the Oklahoma prairie's summers and winters and the Florida bust and his failed banker father's suicide/murder and the Depression and New York City and Columbia and Cambridge University and his mother's betrayals, followed by World War II and the long Cold War and the McCarthy hearings and the Cuban Missile Crisis and Khrushchev (we will bury you!) and the race riots and the long, desperate protests against the war in Vietnam and Laos and Cambodia . . . how is it that this philanderer who made charts of his conquests, a man who married three times and sorely tried all three wives, this binger, this brilliant, blasphemous naysayer, should somehow make it into the hallowed pages of the saints?

The trouble seems to have begun—and ended—with the death of his father when Berryman was eleven. He and his younger brother, Robert, were living with their parents then—John Allyn and Martha (Jill) Smith—in an apartment down on Clearwater Island in Tampa Bay. Before long, Berryman's mother began carrying on an affair with the janitor, while his suicidal father took up with a Cuban woman and found accommodations elsewhere. There were arguments, scenes, recriminations, accusations, and shouts out in the hall beyond the boys' closed bedroom door. Then, early on the morning of Friday, June 26, 1926, John heard his mother's footsteps in the hall before she came into the room to tell the boys that their father was dead. He'd apparently killed himself with a bullet to the chest and lay spreadeagled now in the alley behind the apartment.

Afterwards, Martha and the janitor, twenty years her senior, whose name was John Berryman, married and moved to an apartment in Queens, New York, where John and Robert were informed that their last name was no longer Smith but Berryman.

In time Martha would tell the old geezer that it was time to move out, while she remade herself, telling John—then at Columbia University—to inform his friends that she was not his mother, actually, but his older (and single) sister.

In time, too, Berryman, going over the evidence that he could gather about the death of his father, wondered if indeed his mother and stepfather hadn't killed his father and left the gun near his body. No wonder Berryman would later obsess over the play within a play in Shakespeare's *Hamlet*, where Hamlet's father's death is rehearsed on stage before the usurper king and Hamlet's mother. Once, in fact, Berryman went so far as to invite his mother to hear him lecture on *Hamlet* while he was teaching at Princeton, hoping to finally out his mother with the scene verbally reenacted for her to witness aghast at. But once more, she coolly avoided the well-laid trap, leaving Berryman to pick up the shattered pieces of himself.

The obsession about the father followed him all his life, before, during, and after he composed his four-hundred-plus famous and brilliant Dream Songs. No wonder the last but one of Berryman's published Dream Songs should begin this way:

The marker slants, flowerless, day's almost done,

I stand above my father's grave with rage . . .

I spit upon this dreadful banker's grave

Who shot his heart out in a Florida dawn

O ho alas alas

When will indifference come, I moan & rave. . . .

Which brought to a tentative end what the first Song had begun:

Huffy Henry hid   the day

unappeasable Henry sulked.

There's that linear gap, then, on the very first day of Berryman's nightmare creation: the day he'd tried for so many years to simply hide, when everything changed forever and a departure came, so that, from then on, nothing ever "fell out as it might or ought."

As a boy back in Anadarko, Oklahoma, he'd served each morning at early Mass with Father Boniface, the two of them up there by the small pre-Vatican II altar, intoning the Latin together—*Introibo ad altare Dei*—while six blue-hairs knelt in the pews behind them. And he had been happy. Happy.

Well, that phase was over now. With the death of his father, his other Father had gone too, confined it seemed forever to the shadows, or at least to the irrelevancies of classical literature, by which he would make his living. God had abandoned him, and he in turn was leaving God behind, to make good in any way he could: sex, adulteries, booze, high talk among his intellectual peers about the state of the world and the present perilous state of "God." He read, everything: the classics and the Bible as literature and his worthy contemporaries, and, after a year in England, affected a quasi-British accent spiced with American Jazz speech, which he maintained for the rest of his days. If he had to pay homage, let him pay it to the Greats who deserved it, or at least half-deserved it, considering he would do his damnedest to outshine them all: Hopkins, Housman, Yeats, Eliot, Pound, Auden, and later his friend Saul Bellow and Ralph Ellison and Dylan Thomas and Robert Lowell and Adrienne Rich, making elaborate lists of living poets just to see how he and they were faring with the passage of time.

The trouble was that he was not indifferent to the torments of others. "Hard on the land wears the strong sea," the first Dream Song ends, recalling the beach where his father would swim out and feign his disappearance, thus shaking his son's heart to its core. "And empty grows every bed": it's a line from Bessie Smith's *Empty Bed Blues*, and it reminds us of what only a black woman named Smith (like himself) could sing: that sooner or later every bed indeed grows empty.

"I am obliged to perform in complete darkness," he wrote in one Dream Song, "operations of great delicacy."[67] The real trouble was that he had to perform these operations on himself. And then write them down for others to see what he had discovered in his heart and brain for—thanks to Freudian analysis—this is where his poetry had led him. It's a funny line, as funny as E. E. Cummings's on the demise of Buffalo Bill: "what I want to know is, how do you like your blue-eyed boy now, Mr. Death."[68] Funny, that is, until you see it tattooed on the chest of a young soldier returned from Afghanistan, dead by his own hand.

But here's the rub: even when Berryman went after God most violently, he knew he still owed a tremendous debt to those for whom following that path "cost not less than everything."[69] If Berryman's poems, early and late, are difficult, he sees that they are difficult in the same way that biblical passages (and even their glosses) can be difficult. In the same way, he noted, St. Jerome, having "had difficulties with his biblical commentary," went on to quote from a commentary on the fathers of the church to the effect that, if a passage was obscure (*vide* St. John and Berryman), it was "due to the enormity of the task, the teacher's lack of skills, & the indifference of his listeners."[70] And so on he wrote, in the shadow of the Bible.

And then, as he says, there came a change, a metanoia.

It happened when he was consigned to the locked ward for extreme intoxication as a danger to himself and others. This time he found himself in St. Mary's, a Catholic hospital in Minneapolis in the spring of 1970, where he was informed by Jim Zosel, an Episcopal priest in charge of the group's welfare, that, no, he could not take a taxi over to his classes and teach, because every time he did, he would cajole or command the driver to stop at one of the local bars afterward to refresh himself before returning for rehab. But because Berryman was teaching the Gospel of John that term, the priest volunteered to take over his classes while he recovered.

That was when something deep within him gave way, the fact that someone could actually care enough about this unworthy soul to do such a thing.

And so his recovery began. He joined AA, acted as a sponsor to others, stayed off the booze "each damned day," and began attending weekly Mass, though he remained an acute critical observer of the stylistic shortcomings and content of the priest's homilies in these too-facile post–Vatican II days. He was also assembling poems in a post-*Dream Song* mode, many of them unrhymed quatrains that owed as much to Emily Dickinson as they did to that witty, irreverent French *poète maudit*, Tristan Corbière, who had died of consumption at twenty-nine, and, like Dickinson, was then unknown to the larger literary world beyond.

As for Berryman, he was certainly well known. In fact, he was in demand everywhere, showered with awards and prizes and rave notices in prominent national magazines like *Time* and *Life*. Likewise, from his college days on, he had had his share of love, or at least of Eros. *Love & Fame* he meant to call the new volume, and he was pleased as hell with what he'd already wrought.

And then came the turn, which puzzled, amused, and disturbed the literary critics as well as his fellow poets. It began abruptly with Berryman's "Eleven Addresses to the Lord," which turned the book

Augustine-like completely on its head. For if God was the "slob" he'd complained of four years earlier, the locked ward he now found himself in told him in no uncertain terms who the real slob was.

"Master of beauty," the sequence begins, like Father Hopkins celebrating the all-mastering God as the true Artist, "inimitable contriver" and "endower of Earth so gorgeous & different from the boring Moon."[71] Prayers of praise, then, prayers of thanksgiving. Like the Psalms, but with their own wry sense of humor—gallows humor, perhaps, but funny and vulnerable, those photos of the unforgiving desert landscape of the moon's surface showing him the condition of his own soul. Nothing for it then but to beg for rescue from the prison of himself, rescue by a God it seemed who really cared. "You have come to my rescue again & again," he sang now, "in my impassible, sometimes despairing years."

Oh, he still had questions, as that wily elder Robert Frost who had chided him up at Bread Loaf always had. Given the human condition, he understood now that he would still have questions half an hour after he was dead. Who, for example, could really claim to know the Mystery of God? And, by logical extension, how could one actually come to love the Unknowable? And did we live again after death? It didn't "seem likely / from either the scientific or the philosophical point of view." But who was he to say? One thing was clear: he was surer now than ever that "all things are possible to you."[72] He also understood that he was ready to move on with "gratitude & awe," hoping "to stand until death forever at attention / for any your least instruction or enlightenment." Somehow, he knew the Ineffable would assist him again and yes again, because at the mysterious heart of it all, the Ineffable had revealed itself as Love.

All this was a honeymoon phase between him and God, no doubt: the cry of a brilliant, intense, broken man who had come to admit that he—*he*—needed some deep consolation. He thought of those who had gone before, like St. Germanicus, the Roman officer still in his prime condemned to face the lions in the arena for his faith, who had thrown himself on a raging lion rather than wait, "wishing to pass quickly from a lawless life."[73]

Or St. Polycarp, John the Evangelist's disciple, who had been given the stark choice by the Roman authorities of denying Christ or being burned alive, only to answer thus:

> Eighty & six years have I been his servant,
> and he has done me no harm.
> How can I blaspheme my King who saved me?[74]

Berryman ended his remarkable sequence with yet another prayer, a plea this time, that this same God would somehow make him acceptable too at the end,

> Which then Thou wilt award.
> Cancer, senility, mania,
> I pray I may be ready with my witness.

And life, such as it was, went on. In the winter of '71 he was still at it with yet another set of poems, this time his own version of the Divine Office. It's the "Opus Dei" sequence that opens his final, posthumous volume of poems, *Delusions, Etc.* In it he quoted from five different sources by way of entry, among them Matthew's Gospel (11:17), Chaucer, and Tolstoy's "The Devil," in which Berryman reminded his readers that if Tolstoy's protagonist—for which read himself—"was mentally deranged, everyone is in the same case," the most mentally deranged being those "who see in others indications of insanity they do not notice in themselves."[75]

"With the human exhausted," Helen Vendler once mocked, "Berryman solicited the divine."[76] And the poems he wrote in this new vein, especially in his "Opus Dei" sequence, she insisted, were simply no good. If Berryman had discovered a "newly simple heart" and new visions into the workings of his God,

whatever temporary calm they gave his soul, gave no new life to his
poetry, and the last two poems, particularly ["Vespers" and "Compline"],
are intolerable to read. . . . When he became the redeemed child of God,
his shamefaced vocabulary drooped useless, and no poet can be expected
to invent, all at once and at the end of his life, a convincing new stance,
a new style in architecture along with his change of heart. Berryman's
suicide threw all finally into question—Henry's sly resourcefulness as
much as Berryman's abject faith. In the end, it seems, neither was enough
to get through the day on, and even though a voice divine the storm
allayed, a light propitious shone, this castaway could not avoid another
rising of the gulf to overwhelm him.[77]

But Vendler, when it comes to the religious sensibility, turned a stone
ear on her subject, as with Hopkins, as with Stevens. The truth is that
Berryman wrote out of what he knew, a radically broken man using
all the resources still at his command. One thing was sure: he was not
going to wax ironic and detached in the best Modern or post-Modern
mode. Or at least, knowing himself too well, he was going to try his
damnedest not to. He'd tried that approach with other inmates who had
hit rock bottom and, having heard it all before, they'd detected at once
the buzzing lies and false reconstructions and obfuscations and all the
other—call it what it was—verbal merde.

You, hypocrite lecteur, mon semblable, mon frère. Thus T. S. Eliot, speaking
through the voice of Baudelaire in perhaps the central poem of the
twentieth century, *The Waste Land*, one that stands like a steel crossbar
behind Berryman's late religious poems, poetic fragments shored up
against his own ruins.

So where was Berryman when he wrote these fragments, then? Where
was the world? And where in all that hell was God? "Adorns my crossbar
Your high frenzied Son," he wrote, much as St. Paul had written to his
people in "Sin City Corinth" nearly two millennia earlier, having sworn,
after his failure to convince the Stoics and Cynics at Athens—the Sorbonne

and Cambridge of its day—to preach the heart of that strange, shattering mystery: Christ crucified, a divine foolishness wiser than human wisdom and a weakness stronger than human strength (1 Cor. 1:25) , the witness of the divine Word that had remained "mute over catcalls."[78]

"Gunfire & riot" were fanning "thro' new Detroit" even as Berryman sweated over his final sequence. Protesters were being tried, imprisoned, and fined, while others—four college students at Kent State—were being gunned down for refusing to participate any longer in the madness of Vietnam. The homeless were still homeless and the hungry went on being hungry. And, yes, his own body was failing and, yes, he had made mistakes and, yes, he was a human wreck, but he would bear witness in a terrible time as best he could. He hoped and prayed that that heretic Origen was right after all and that hell was "empty / Or will be at apocatastasis," that is, at the end of time. Human failure—sin—seemed inevitable, given who and what we were. And, yes, no doubt we would suffer for it "now & later / but not forever, dear friends & brothers!"[79] Not forever.

I like to think of John Berryman as the patron saint of purgatory, shoulders hunched, still climbing on all fours the steep inclines of those mountains Dante imagined for us, toward that distant summit shimmering in light, relieved to know he could sin no more. He's walking beside Hart Crane, and they're both listening to Crane's distant "sapphire flutings" that Berryman recalls now in the closing lines of his evening prayer just before he lays his weary head down.

He's in Minneapolis as he writes these lines, and it's midwinter and he and his family and all the citizens of this earthly city are journeying on. And then, suddenly, he recalls a moment when the sky shone red. Just now, he knows, there are "no fair bells in this city," and, in truth, his house is as cold and fireless as himself. Still, he will try and manage to ask his real Father that, even if he should fall from some terrifying height, God in His infinite mercy will send his angels to save him. In the meantime, here in this wintry nick, he will have to content himself, as others have, to wait out his own dark night.

12
DIFFICULT HENRY AND
THE DREAM SONGS

H it's hard, Henry tells us, and he may as well be talking about *The Dream Songs*. I've been reading them now for thirty years, along with *The Cantos* and *Paterson*, all of which make *The Waste Land* look from this vantage almost transparent, like a private bit of grumbling, as Eliot long afterward himself said of his poem. Even *The Bridge* looks more pliable with the passage of the years. Admittedly, some of the Songs—like the notorious 4th, with Henry in a restaurant moaning over a beauty sitting at a table across from him, yield their meaning quickly:

> Filling her compact & delicious body
> with chicken páprika, she glanced at me
> twice.
> Fainting with interest, I hungered back
> and only the fact of her husband & four other people
> kept me from springing on her. . . .[80]

Et cetera, et cetera. One gets the point here rather quickly. But more often the effect of reading a Dream Song is a mixture of lightning clarity followed by lines that shut clam-tight against the inquiring mind, refusing to reveal themselves.

"Dream Songs," Berryman called them. Lyrics consisting of three six-line stanzas, usually with three rhymes to a stanza, an iambic pentameter at the core of the poem, but with short lines (some consisting of a phrase or even a single word) punctuating the poem. But there's also the seeming nonlinear illogicality of the dreams to contend with, something both vivid and mysterious, emblematic, a scenario that disturbs or signifies before it is understood. Writing poems, Freud has told us, is after all a form of daydreaming, a place where the conscious mind and the unconscious meet and cross.

But there's a further difficulty. *The Dream Songs* is a single poem, Berryman insisted, and not discrete lyrics, any more than a single sonnet in a sonnet sequence tells the whole story. The Songs build on one another, creating a narrative and a character, as they call back and forth across the pages to each other. Themes, preoccupations, images, voices: all these gather force until a psychodrama is presented for our understanding. The pieces, Henry tells us in his famous 29th Song, are each hacked from a single body, and hidden, but in a way so that they may be found. But as with Pound and Williams and Faulkner and a host of others, it takes sleuthing, and in the absence of an overvoice to put it all together, we will have to act as our own sleuths.

Cagey Henry has told us as much in the opening line of the opening poem. "Huffy Henry hid." Hid what? Well, the day for one thing. And the day, we learn, in Dream Song 76, the day Henry meant to hide, is the one on which he suffered an irreversible loss: a day many years before, in Tampa, when his mother told him and his little brother that their daddy had taken himself away forever. One thing Henry means to do someday, then, is rejoin this father,

who dared so long agone leave me.
A bullet on a concrete stoop
close by a smothering southern sea
spreadeagled on an island, by my knee. . . .

But there are issues to attend to before Henry can leave the scene
at the end of the Fifth Act: a wife, a son, a daughter, a mother to take
care of (and without a father to instruct or help him along the way),
along with battles and a living to wage and lose, and a long poem to
somehow get written, in which he has for too many years hidden behind
his meaning. Well, it's time now to come out and talk.

But how does Henry talk to us, after all? Consider two of the original
seventy-seven Songs. Not the more famous ones, like 4 or 16 or 18 or 29
or 77, but Songs 72 and 73. The first has received no critical attention,
while the second one has. When Berryman read from his *Dream Songs* at
the Guggenheim in late 1963, he had just decided to print seventy-six
Dream Songs. The book was already in press when he added a new poem
to bring the collection up to seventy-seven: "The Elder Presences." He
wrote this Song on December 19, while he and his wife and their one-
year-old daughter were staying in Washington, DC, with his mother.

Four weeks earlier President Kennedy had been shot as he paraded
in an open car through Dallas, and a shocked Berryman had watched
from a television at the Chelsea Hotel in New York—and then, in
succession, the riderless horse, the two-year-old John saluting his father,
Oswald captured, Oswald gunned down by Jack Ruby in the Dallas
police station. All of that Berryman had written about in another poem,
breaking his obsession with the Dream Songs long enough to give voice
to his outrage and stunned grief.

Now, in December, in Washington, in "The Elder Presences," he
returned to his Songs, the state of a bereft nation as much on his mind
as it had been on the mind of Whitman, who had also been living in this
city when another president had been shot and killed a hundred years

before. Behind both events for despairing Henry—as for others—there is the still-unresolved issue of the treatment of basic civil rights withheld. Living just across the street from the Supreme Court Building, "Best-looking place in town," Henry crows in Song 200, written the same week, another Song that evokes the same scene and Henry's outrage and grief with justice aborted or justice withheld. "It's Christmas," Henry says there,

> and *brrr*
> in Washington. My wife's candle is out
> for John F. Kennedy

> and the law rushes like mud but the park is white
> with a heavy fall for ofays & for dark,
> let's exchange blue-black kisses
> for the fate of the Man who was not born today,
> clashing our tinsel, by the terrible tree
> whereon he really hung, for you & me.

Across the street from Henry's modest apartment, in a little park on the grounds of the Supreme Court, Henry pushes his little daughter from a tree swing in Dream Song 72, a tree bare and "disastered" by the curse of winter. From here he can see the statues of some of the former Supreme Court justices. The "high statues of the wise," Henry calls them, and for a moment, disoriented Henry—"drunk"—thinks of them as black, staring out upon the apocalyptic scene, passing mute judgment on the world.

There's the shadow of a lynching hanging over this as over so many of the Songs: "burnt-cork" blackface Henry crucified, Henry treed, like a "coon," like a black man. The curse of Henry, who knows how far he is separated from his brothers by the history of America, is a history as old, really, as the story of Cain and Abel. After all these millennia of evolution, after all these "chirrs & leapings," after so much human effort expended, where is it we have arrived, if we have indeed arrived anywhere, Henry asks, What got us here to this state of things, saddled down with self-consciousness and no sure answers to our questions? Certainly not the striving after good. Teilhard de Chardin and the omega point of human evolution notwithstanding, we seem to belong to another pattern altogether, and not one where Henry feels any more at home than, say, tiny Thomas Hardy did.

Perhaps greed got us to where we are, the going after one's naked self-interest. Whichever, the gods of this Washington garden are not saying one way or the other. It may well be that for every push forward, there's a falling back again, and that the answer Henry is looking for is to be found in his little girl swinging first out and then back, out and back. A leap forward and up, a rising, and then, alas, the inevitable falling. A progress of sorts, followed by a murder. Henry's life. Everybody's.

But there is another method, as Berryman has already told us in the last of the three epigrams that lead off *The Dream Songs*. And so Berryman turns in Dream Song 73 to another group of Elder Presences and another garden: to the Zen masters, Hosokawa chief among them, who built the Zen garden at Ryoan-ji in the old Japanese capital in Kyoto half a millennium before. "The most perfect & satisfying garden even in Japan," Berryman crowed after he'd visited the garden with its

fifteen changeless stones in their five worlds
with a shelving of moving moss

in the summer of '57.

I do survive beside the garden I

came seven thousand mile the other way
supplied of engines all to see, to see,

Henry tells us.

For if death is the gigantic figure looming in Dream Song 72, Henry has found a way for the I—the I that begins and ends the last line of the first stanza: "I do survive beside the garden I"—to go on surviving after the shucking of this mortal coil, and the answer is, for him as for Keats before him, to be found in the changeless world of art. Wars, assassinations, age, cancer, senility, yes, but over against all that: this "austere . . . sea rectangular of sand by the oiled mud wall, / . . . granite sand, grey," a pattern of fifteen stones that changes depending on where the reader of the garden stands, bringing to mind "the thought of the ancient maker priest," a man long since turned to dust, but whose thought, whose "stone & sand thought" has been found worthy to live on. Art abides, hopelessly Romantic Henry hopes, somehow beyond all "awes & weathers," and, should even the mud and sand garden somehow be destroyed, there would still be the *idea* of the Garden in the mind of the beholder. If loss occurs, Henry can finally say—and he knows full well it does—it occurs elsewhere and not, please God, here.

Dream Song 74 continues where 73 left off, though it is difficult in truth to speak of a development. Developments do not become Henry, nor does Henry appear to trust in developments. Time is the enemy; time expels from the garden. Time brings with it its own undoing. "Henry hates the world," 74 begins, and we are right back to 1, or 16, or 72 or 73, as Henry circles the original wound that will not heal. For art itself is also a double-edged gift, taking from the artist even as it returns the pain, transformed:

> Henry hates the world. What the world to Henry
> did will not bear thought.
> Feeling no pain,
> Henry stabbed his arm and wrote a letter
> explaining how bad it had been
> in this world.

This, it seems, is exactly what these Dream Songs are: letters to the world that Henry hates for having unhanded him, especially for the horror of unlove, as with one's mother, pal. Not much one can do about such a turn of events, Mr. Bones, except sing on, bulb on, in the dawn, mastering one's art, and "tasting all the secret bits of life"—which may be a consolation of sorts, at least for some, after all.

And yet, and yet. . . . There's desolation, and then there's another take on such desolation. I've studied, pored over, laughed, cringed, and cried with John Berryman now for the past four decades and more, learning what I could from him as one more poet writing in an American idiom. Add to this, since I have written of the lives (and suicides) of both Hart Crane and Berryman, is the one major question I am left with: Would I be willing to jump to my death, as these two men did, if I could be assured of their fame? Wasn't that one of the offers Matthew's Gospel tells us Satan made to Jesus when he took him up atop the temple in Jerusalem and showed him all the glory that could be his, if he just trusted in God's angels and jumped (Matt. 4:5–6)?

Of course we're talking fantasy here. But still, how does one answer such a question? And what have I come away with after all these years of writing about those lives as a biographer and poet who ultimately identifies himself as embracing the Catholic faith? You do what you can, I keep telling myself, write when you can, and try to remember each and every day to thank God for the blessings he sends your way, soldiering on like those anonymous monks copying out the sacred texts on those sheets of vellum in the monastic scriptorium and facing the long hours of loneliness in their cells. Or, like dear Fr. Hopkins, writing out those poems of his to no one in particular, in the face of his own isolation, there at a small desk in his upstairs room facing a small garden glimmering in the Dublin gray of 85–86 St. Stephen's Green, grading paper after paper, until at last the light descended.

13
WHAT LIES BEYOND LANGUAGE

n Wilfred Owen's "Strange Meeting" we are confronted with a cold, mud-slimed trench indistinguishable from one of Dante's malebolges that line this district of hell, where the poet confronts the figure of the man he ran through with a bayonet the night before. Owen would have found the title for his poem in his copy of Shelley, there in that strange, neglected poem "The Revolt of Islam." There the speaker, run through with a spear, looks up to find the other, the stranger, stricken with horror at what he has just done:

> And one, whose spear had pierced me, leaned beside
> With quivering lips and humid eyes; and all
> Seemed like some brothers on a journey wide
> Gone forth, whom now strange meeting did befall
> In a strange land round one whom they might call
> Their friend, their chief, their father. . . .[81]

Might have, that is, in another time and another place. One encounters the other, the compound, familiar ghost, the one one fears, the enemy, met now in a nightmare, phosphorescent sleep in the rat-infested trenches of the Great War. The other: in this instance a man without a name whom he has killed in battle, in a place where ignorant armies clash by night. Perhaps the speaker is dead himself now, or drugged with exhaustion, where the Dantesque landscape of two worlds—hell and France—have become much like one another. Perhaps it is a nightmare only, from which the poet will awaken to find himself back in a living hell. In any event it is the time between, a time in which to let the other finally have his say, as there was no time in the epic sweep of battle, when the man tried to parry the blow, or was too terrified to do so, or perhaps too tired, wanting it over, hungry for the long sleep so long denied him.

Nothing has been lost, the speaker tries to assuage the stranger whom he recognizes as both stranger *and* as friend. And the stranger? Nothing except my life, and what I might have done, and what I might have warned against. And now we realize that the stranger *is* the Self, speaking one's own deepest dreams deferred now forever. Like Owen, who would take a machine-gun bullet to the forehead as he tried to get his men across a canal that November 1918, in the last days of the war, like a tired mother hovering over her little ones, the man he killed might have gone

> hunting wild
> After the wildest beauty in the world,
> Which lies not calm in eyes, or braided hair,
> But mocks the steady running of the hour,
> And if it grieves, grieves richlier than here.
> For by my glee might many men have laughed,
> And of my weeping something had been left,
> Which must die now. I mean the truth untold,
> The pity of war, the pity war distilled.
> Now men will go content with what we spoiled,

Or, discontent, boil bloody, and be spilled. . . .
I am the enemy you killed, my friend.
I knew you in this dark: for so you frowned
Yesterday through me as you jabbed and killed.
I parried; but my hands were loath and cold.
Let us sleep now. . . .[82]

And here's Berryman, a.k.a. Henry House, likewise meeting the dead
there in the night-reaches, in this instance his friend and adversary the
poet-critic Randall Jarrell, dead at fifty-one, young even for that age
of lost poets, though not as young as either Plath or Sexton. "There's
a small chance" that Randall's death was "an accident," a chastened
Robert Lowell wrote Elizabeth Bishop a week after Jarrell walked into a
speeding car in an underpass weeks after cutting his wrists, but "I think
it was suicide, and so does everyone else, who knew him well."[83]

"In the night-reaches dreamed he of better graces," Berryman writes
by way of elegy, having in his mind's eye entered the long tunnels now
of death himself. The struggle at long last over, in death he, too, can
dream of hosting the compound, familiar ghost of Randall and Yeats and
Roethke and so many others who have preceded him into the unfamiliar
world

of liberations, and beloved faces,
such as now ere dawn he sings.
It would not be easy, accustomed to these things,
to give up the old world, but he could try;
let it all rest, have a good cry.

Let Randall rest, whom your self-torturing
cannot restore one instant's good to, rest:
he's left us now.
The panic died and in the panic's dying
so did my old friend. I am headed west

also, also, somehow.
In the chambers of the end we'll meet again
I will say Randall, he'll say Pussycat
and all will be as before
when as we sought, among the beloved faces,
eminence and were dissatisfied with that
and needed more.[84]

Or consider Hopkins there in his bleak, cell-like room on the third
story of the makeshift school off St. Stephen's Green, parrying with the
Stranger, Jacob's Angel, or something far more terrifying:

Not, I'll not, carrion comfort, Despair, not feast on thee;
Not untwist—slack they may be—these last strands of man
In me ór, most weary, cry *I can no more.* I can;
Can something, hope, wish day come, not choose not to be.

But ah, but O thou terrible, why wouldst thou rude on me
Thy wring-world right foot rock? lay a lionlimb against me? scan
With darksome devouring eyes my bruisèd bones? and fan,
O in turns of tempest, me heaped there; me frantic to avoid thee and
    flee?

    Why? That my chaff might fly; my grain lie, sheer and clear.
Nay in all that toil, that coil, since (seems) I kissed the rod,
Hand rather, my heart lo! lapped strength, stole joy, would laugh, chéer.
Cheer whom though? The hero whose heaven-handling flung me, fóot
    tród
Me? or me that fought him? O which one? is it each one? That night,
    that year
Of now done darkness I wretch lay wrestling with (my God!) my God.

A cat and mouse game, then, something in the priest rebelling with that rebel will of his against . . . whom? The enemy, the stranger? The friend? His own dark Doppelgänger? The crucified Christ, hanging by his mangled hands from the rugged crossbeam? And Hopkins, coming out of the darkness of the long night to catch himself likewise broken, uttering the opening line of the forty-second psalm, "My God, My God, why have you forsaken me?" uttered now first as a cry of pain, and then as a sign of utter amazement, the words chiming perfectly with his Master's.

Consider, too, Seamus Heaney's pilgrim on Station Island, after the long fast and the prayers, suddenly coming across a dead friend, one more victim of the old wars between Protestant and Catholic in Northern Ireland back thirty years ago. In lines of exquisite terza rima, Heaney evokes the shock and horror of seeing his dead friend standing there at the edge of the water, between two worlds. "Easy now," the dead man reassures him, still carrying the open wound to his head. "It's only me. You've seen men as raw / after a football match." So with Homer, so with Virgil and Propertius and Seneca down the ages, so with Dante, as the familiar dead across the waters unsettle and comfort in the strange, narcotic plush of the poem's hypnotic music.

Or, on the lighter side, this riff on the landscapes of the afterlife by Berryman's Henry, sharing a martini with St. Peter at the pearly gates before the verdict is read aloud and the landscape undergoes a radical shift:

Peter's not friendly. He gives me sideways looks.
The architecture is far from reassuring.
I feel uneasy.
A pity,—the interview began so well:
I mentioned fiendish things, he waved them away
and sloshed out a martini

strangely needed. We spoke of indifferent matters—
God's health, the vague hell of the Congo,
John's energy,

anti-matter matter. I felt fine.

Then a change came backward. A chill fell.

Talk slackened,

died, and began to give me sideways looks.

'Christ,' I thought 'what now?' and would have askt for another

but didn't dare.

I feel my application   failing. It's growing dark,

some other sound is overcoming. His last words are:

'We betrayed me.'

Whoever the "we" is here, whoever the "me," all pronominal references undergo a terrifying metamorphosis into death's dissolution.

I notice this lately as my own poems insist on moving in a direction other than what I would have supposed. In truth, I would have thought I'd be reaching something like the penumbra of some Paradiso, some shadow of Stevens's "palm at the end of the mind," a kind of contentment such as I feel in my life each day. But the poems seem stranger and stranger to their own creator. Of course there's a precedent for this among my masters: Yeats finding himself in death as the hero Cuchulain, surrounded now by strangers knitting shrouds, cowards all of them, as I suspect Yeats feared at heart he might have felt after the trials of the Easter 1916 uprising, which saw the leaders of the rebellion lined up against a wall in Dublin Castle one after the other and shot.

Or Hart Crane in the bell tower in Mexico that spring of 1932, pulling lustily at the rope, and wondering who at the last he might summon to his orphic songs, if anyone was listening. Or Eliot in "Little Gidding," set in London during the German Luftwaffe attacks, being warned by the "compound, familiar ghost" (including Yeats, who had died the year before) what the dreadful options for both their futures might well be.

Forty years ago, I tried an experiment on myself. Go down into yourself, a friend had advised, down and down in your electric Kool-Aid acid art-deco elevator, down to Gamma Level—wherever Gamma was—and see who might be waiting at the door to greet you there. So he put me under a light hypnotic trance and I proceeded down the elevator. A short time later the elevator door opened and I saw someone standing there, someone who at first I did not recognize. In truth I had half-expected to meet one of my old friends I had spent the better part of my life writing about: Hopkins or Williams or Lowell or Berryman or Hart Crane. Or, if not them, Stevens or Frost or—as on an earlier trip— my father driving his pay loader across some old cemetery.

Instead, there was a tallish man standing there in clothes dating back to the 1850s. He had a five o'clock shadow, it seemed, and his eyes glowed amber. He seemed to be in his mid-forties. Who was it, my friend asked? *Baudelaire,* I said. Charles Baudelaire, the French poet. *And I don't even know French.*

Is he speaking? My friend asked. He was, but his lips weren't moving, which made it all the stranger.

What was he saying?

Later I wrote down what he said, or what I thought he said, and netted the strangest poem I've ever been offered. "Clear your head," he advised,

> and pay attention to these presences
> who throng about you. They are friends,
> strange friends, true, whom One has directed
> here to you. Let the hyenas bear their fangs,
> snapping at what they do not understand. They have
> their appointed time, *mon frère,* as you have yours.
> Then ceased, and faded back, was gone.[85]

Something offered, then, strange as it seems: the music of the dead, where each step out into the white spaces remains uncertain and yet desired: the attempt to net the strangeness of language, and the even deeper strangeness of what lies beyond the sound of words themselves.

III
POETRY IN A
POST-CHRISTIAN
AGE

14
CHARISM AND THE LITERARY IMAGINATION

When I began teaching literature and poetry back in the mid-1960s, I had no idea that I would someday be in dialogue with so many others—many of them theologians—concerning such fundamental issues as the various charisms that together make up the idea of a Catholic university, for the subject is so vast and so nuanced at the same time that it's important to pay close attention as we listen to each other wrestling with these issues.

Let's begin by examining the idea of charism, one definition of which suggests a spiritual gift that helps define what one discerns one has been called to do in entering the Mystery of Creation. Since I know that I do not possess the special intellectual charism, say, of St. Thomas Aquinas, to synthesize a reality I only dimly understand, being all too often another conflicted citizen in our own postmodern, perhaps post-everything historical moment, I will have to examine the question of the Catholic literary imagination in a way that makes sense to me. I hope this will resonate with others as well, since charism is not an exclusively Catholic—or even Christian—matter. The issues involved here suggest a task that would require a staggering multitude of intellectual and personal lenses, each having its own language, one that in large part also identifies who we are.

We can begin this inquiry by acknowledging a shared sense of what brings us together when we approach such a topic from a range of perspectives—including, say, those within the horizon of a Roman Catholic university, among them theologians, political scientists, biologists, physicists, economists, psychologists, historians, to say nothing of professors of literature. Across such a broad spectrum, one might find a surprisingly shared sense of understanding regarding this matter, and by extension, perhaps even a common sense of what this might suggest of our "mission" within such a context. What is involved in such a conversation, it seems, is the willingness to listen to the other, but also to exchange, clarify, and, yes, expand what we understand to be our own special charisms. This requires that we seek to understand how each of our voices shares in and adds to the available stock of what we see as the central mystery of existence. For us, this will mean a continued prayerful discernment to better understand and share the gifts we have been given, because that is what Love does.

I see myself as fully engaged in the creative work of the imagination in my work, whether as poet, biographer, memoirist, critic, or scholar, and this surely includes my work as someone who has taught at the university level for over fifty years. I was first introduced to the Catholic literary imagination as a young man. After years in a Catholic parish and high school, and a year discerning whether I had a vocation to the priesthood, I spent four years, between 1958 and 1962, at Manhattan College in the Riverdale section of the Bronx, a Catholic college run by the LaSalle Christian Brothers. It was here that, after first considering majoring in psychology and then in medieval philosophy, I opted at the last moment for English and American studies, my real loves, taking a total of 156 credits in theology and the humanities, including Latin and Greek. I simply could not get enough of what was being offered me, and I spent every extra dollar I had on cheap paperbacks of everything from Plato and Aristotle to Piers Plowman and the church fathers.

What Manhattan College gave me was a knowledge and a freedom that my parents, products of the Depression, never had, and that I vowed even then to pass on to others: a visionary synthesis of the Great Books, a knowledge that I have seen fade and crumble with time in both our society and the academic community, to be replaced too often with the chitter of critical languages and meta-theories, which usually enjoy a shelf life of a dozen or so years before they themselves are set aside for the next trending fashion, each new approach heralded as "the latest and greatest" new knowledge ever to be packaged.

What I was offered back then was four years of cornerstone courses in the Western tradition, beginning with the Egyptians and Babylonians, on through the Greeks and Romans, then on to the Middle Ages, the Renaissance, the Reformation and Counter-Reformation, the rationalists of the Enlightenment, European Romanticism, the American experience, and the twentieth century, including World Wars I and II. Part of this curriculum included, each semester, four related courses in philosophy, history, literature, and the arts (music, architecture, sculpture, and painting).

Nights I worked at my father's gas station pumping gas, and when that failed, I shredded highly classified government documents in a locked room in some apartment complex in Mineola, or stacked shelves in two branches of the A&P on the "six to eleven" shift, after which I listened to Mozart, Beethoven, and Rimsky-Korsakov on an old 78 rpm Victrola. Those classes at Manhattan, focused on the Western tradition, were then and have remained the key to my understanding of the literary tradition and—as if I had looked up at the stars without fully understanding it at the time—gave me a glimpse of what the human imagination is capable of.

After that I went on to Colgate University for my master's in English, taking courses in everything from the Jacobean playwrights to Edmund

Burke and Gibbon and Jane Austen, as well as Ralph Waldo Emerson, Thomas Carlyle, E. A. Robinson, and Robert Frost, and meeting writers as diverse as Robert Creeley and Michael Harper and Isaac Bashevis Singer. And then four years at the Graduate Center of the City University, where I found my ideal mentor in Allen Mandelbaum, translator of Virgil and Dante and Ovid and Homer, as well as of Ungaretti, Montale, Quasimodo, and Giudici.

Of course, there were and are and always will be gaps in one's education, no matter how much one tries to fill them in, for each subject as it is examined seems to widen and deepen into a galaxy of its own, and, inevitably, within that galaxy, other galaxies begin to reveal themselves. I know too that what I constructed over those four years was only a skein of what constitutes the ever-expanding realities of our multivalent worlds.

For one thing, as the '60s made clearer as they unfolded, I came to see how relatively few women had been incorporated into the Western tradition I'd been offered at an all-men's college, as well as how little there was of Asian, Middle Eastern, African, Latin American, as well as Native American, African American, Asian American, and Hispanic American history and culture included in my courses. The result was that not fewer and fewer, but more and more questions arose over the years as to how these competing and yet complementary voices were to be incorporated into a core curriculum that by most standards was already overflowing. New balances would have to be created, new knowledges, new thresholds, new anatomies discovered.

Less than a decade after I graduated from Manhattan, the Great Books Core there had been revised, redirected, deboned, filleted, and finally abandoned. Most students felt they'd been inundated with too many one- and two- and three-credit courses in order to include St. Anselm and Abelard, or Bach and Mozart, or Fra Angelico and the Post-Impressionists. Then, too, there was the question of relevance, which bubbled to the surface or came as the necessary aftershocks of America's involvement in Vietnam and the civil rights movement and women's rights.

"Freedom" to choose one's electives, the freedom to express oneself, the distrust of anyone over thirty: all of these almost overnight became the new norm, though—since I'd already left the safety of the academic airport a decade earlier, even as it was being encircled as Dien Bien Phu and Khe San and Columbia University and, later, Saigon would be surrounded—I continued with my pre-1962 dream of filling in the gaps in my education with graduate studies and teaching and my own scholarship for the next six or more decades.

"Let a thousand flowers bloom," I remember one of my white-haired senior colleagues at the University of Massachusetts mumbling over and over back in the 1970s, as the old core unwound and was replaced with newer, more flexible cores. Of course, when he said it, it was with a mixture of disdain and despair as even the basic core that had replaced the earlier, more detailed one came under withering fire and dismemberment, again to be replaced by exemptions in the humanities and English for football players and other athletic icons and a barrage of electives for everyone that took the place of a center that no longer seemed to be able to hold itself together.

There were, of course, many reasons for this turnaround, both by the students, for whom the new chant was relevance, relevance, and more relevance, and by the professors themselves, who were eager to teach their specialties wherever possible, especially in an age of "publish or perish." Another catchword then, as now, was diversity, or the necessary inclusion of many of those voices that had until then been excluded or overlooked in the cultural demographics of the time. Some experiments that incorporated the new voices fared well and grew in a time of radical experimentation, while others faded or overnight were dropped from the curriculum altogether, among the casualties being not only the new experiments but many of the traditional courses as well.

For thirty-two years, from 1968 until 2000, I taught at the University of Massachusetts, and then, approaching my sixtieth birthday, I decided that if change was in the landscape, I was going to have to act, and act soon. And so, after an eight-day spring retreat with the Jesuits in March of 1999, I decided—or God decided for me—that I should teach at Boston College. Which made sense, of course, for though I had never been on the Boston College campus, this change would enable me to work within what I hoped would be a viable Catholic and Jesuit intellectual and literary tradition.

And yet, while I have seen many strong signs of a Catholic charism at Boston College—especially in the fields of theology, philosophy, and history, to name just three—I did not find it flourishing in my own field of English literature. Perhaps I was naïve to expect it, as if I had thought I might find Fr. Bing Crosby walking across campus and singing to himself while the Bells of St. Mary's chimed in the spring air.

What I have found, ironically, among many Catholic institutions of higher learning is that, while the campuses indeed invite the "other" with enthusiasm to sit at the table, the table itself, as far as the Catholic Christian literary tradition goes, has too often been stripped almost bare, so that the very idea of a "Catholic literary imagination" has been shunted more and more to the side, until it seems to have virtually disappeared. This is a tragic shortcoming, finally, because topics like the sacramental understanding of the world in terms of beauty and justice are surely worthy of our consideration, especially in a time when images of death and broken bodies and random acts of violence inundate our music and dance halls and movie theaters and television screens until they have become the new normal, where ideas like mercy and love and forgiveness and commitment to the other often give rise to feelings of embarrassment.

Many individuals would be willing to admit that there's a profound richness to the Catholic artistic and literary tradition. Consider, on the popular level, Fr. Robert Barron's engrossing video series *Catholicism*. But so much of that broad and deep tradition goes untapped here at our own

Catholic universities. In a time of multi-pluralisms, this tradition, which has undergirded our Catholic universities for seven hundred years, is frequently ignored, even as an option or elective to be offered to our students.

Is it because this extraordinary tradition is too often taken as a historical museum piece or perhaps even as an embarrassment? Have we indeed moved into a post-Catholic-university phase where the mission of the Catholic university to support, on some level, a Catholic literary tradition is simply ignored? When I look at our own Catholic Studies program here, I see that of the half dozen or so courses in literature with a Catholic literary component offered over the past decade, only one is still offered, and that of the four professors of English who taught these courses, two are retired, one is deceased, and one is left like Ishmael to tell the story.

But are not Paul and Augustine, Dante and John of the Cross, Hildegard of Bingen and St. Thomas Aquinas, Teresa of Avila and Thérèse of Lisieux—all participants in a great tradition and an open-ended experiment—worthy of our study and of passing their knowledge and wisdom on to our students? Add to this mix Chaucer and Shakespeare, Robert Southwell, Richard Crashaw, Cervantes and Herbert and Hopkins, T. S. Eliot and David Jones and Charles Péguy, Chesterton and Graham Greene and Flannery O'Connor, along with Bach and Palestrina, da Vinci, Michelangelo, and Caravaggio.

Then consider the multitude of writers from Hardy and Yeats, Pound and Hart Crane, William Carlos Williams and Stevens, Faulkner and Hemingway, and on to Willa Cather and William Kennedy and Cormac McCarthy, Kazantzakis, Tolstoy, Dostoevsky, Sartre, Camus, Simon Weil, and so many others who have borrowed from or argued for or against this tradition in their own work. Looked at in this light, is this not a great treasure trove that, if not honored, has at least been ransacked, the stained glass smashed and the great murals ripped from their walls and only the shards left behind? Ah, but what bright shards they are!

Perhaps it is time not only to consider the question of social justice, which would surely have a strong following, but to consider as well the question of beauty, the splendors of nature seen through a sacramental lens: the beauty that Péguy and Rilke and Hopkins and David Jones and W. H. Auden and Flannery O'Connor and T. S. Eliot and Thomas Merton and Hans Urs von Balthasar, among others, have shown us.

In the years I taught at Boston College, I have brought in aspects of the Catholic literary imagination for the simple reason that those images keep coming up again and again of their own accord. So, for example, if I teach Yeats's "The Second Coming," written in the midst of the Irish Troubles, how can I avoid talking about the idea of Christ's second coming, along with the images of the mystery of the Sphinx and the concept of the Jungian *Spiritus Mundi*, and how Yeats has reworked that material here, where Christian teleology and hope give way to the idea of the unending desertlike eternal return?

Surely some revelation is at hand;
Surely the Second Coming is at hand.
The Second Coming! Hardly are those words out
When a vast image out of Spiritus Mundi
Troubles my sight: a waste of desert sand;
A shape with lion body and the head of a man,
A gaze blank and pitiless as the sun,
Is moving its slow thighs, while all about it
Wind shadows of the indignant desert birds.

The darkness drops again but now I know
That twenty centuries of stony sleep
Were vexed to nightmare by a rocking cradle,
And what rough beast, its hour come round at last,
Slouches towards Bethlehem to be born?[86]

Something of this deeper, sacramental understanding of our world is what I'd love to see brought back to our imaginations on a regular basis. With this in mind, I've tried to create at least one course, which has been fully subscribed every year since I began offering it. I called it "God and the Imagination," and it's divided into three parts, following the *Spiritual Exercises* and Dante's *Divine Comedy*. First come the Hell Variations, or the going down ever more deeply, where we focus on the opening and closing cantos of the *Inferno*. Luca Signorelli's images in the cathedral at Orvieto provide vivid images of the end time and of the Antichrist, but so, too, do images of trench warfare, the Malebolge of Dante, and images of the Holocaust and the massive bombings of population centers from Guernica and London, Coventry and Dresden, up through Hiroshima and beyond. Among the poems we look at are Wilfred Owen's "Strange Meeting" and Isaac Rosenberg's "Break of Day in the Trenches," as well as Anthony Hecht's incredibly dark poem "More Light! More Light!" From there we consider Emily Dickinson's "I heard a fly buzz when I died," Thomas Hardy's "The Convergence of the Twain," and Philip Larkin's "Aubade," journeys that stare into the imagined Abyss. Then we turn to the postapocalyptic journey in Cormac McCarthy's *The Road*, to see how a father tries to provide for his young son even when all hope seems lost.

From that point, we move back to Fr. Hopkins's Sonnets of Desolation & Recovery: "Spelt from Sybil's Leaves," "To seem the stranger," "I wake and feel," "No worst, there is none," and "Carrion Comfort," read in conjunction with Psalm 22 and Christ's cry of dereliction from the cross. And then it's *The Waste Land* and the post–World War I landscape, as pockmarked and bomb-blasted as the landscape of the soul in a time of travail—Dante's *selva oscura*, his dark woods.

But this is not the end of that journey. We shift gears, as it were, to consider the "upslope" of hope, and here it's on to the *Purgatorio*, that long journey of the pilgrim, focusing on six of Dante's cantos, then pausing to look at Robert Lowell's renderings of Dante's last-breath

196 THE MYSTERY OF IT ALL

penitent on the battlefield, as well as parts of Hopkins's "The Wreck of the Deutschland" and the cry of the nuns in the midst of that shipwreck. Then it's Marie Howe's "The Star Market," and the presence of Christ in the humblest of places. Next comes William Kennedy's *Ironweed* and the redemptive journey back home, in this case occurring during the triduum of Halloween, All Saints, and All Souls in Depression-ridden Albany, 1938. From that point we return to Eliot, this time examining his "Journey of the Magi" and "Ash Wednesday."

The seminar continues by turning to the journals of Thomas Merton from the late 1930s until his death in the fall of 1968, a tragedy that occurred while he was attending an international conference of monks in Bangkok. And then on to Merton's contemporary Flannery O'Connor, with such classic short stories as "A Good Man Is Hard to Find," "The River," "The Life You Save May Be Your Own," "A Stroke of Good Fortune," "The Artificial Nigger," "Good Country People," and "The Displaced Person." From there we move on to John Berryman, with ten of his bleakest Dream Songs, in which he questions the ways of God and the ways of humanity, before we move to the humbler, searching sequence he wrote while in recovery, his "Eleven Addresses to the Lord."

Finally, it's on to the *Paradiso* and glimpses of heaven and the possibilities of transfigurative change. Here, we look at Hopkins's sonnets of celebration, including "God's Grandeur," "As kingfishers catch fire," "The Windhover," "Pied Beauty," and "Hurrahing in Harvest," "That Nature is a Heraclitean Fire and the Comfort of the Resurrection" and the message of his last, very quiet poem, "To R. B." And then it's back to Eliot and his "Little Gidding," the final sequence of *Four Quartets*, a poem of profound hope composed in the midst of the German bombings of London in 1940 where, in spite of everything, he evokes *The Cloud of Unknowing* and Julian of Norwich's mantra that "All shall be well, and all manner of things shall be well."

From there we focus on four of Dante's *Paradiso* cantos with Beatrice and Mary and Benedict and the amassing of the whole harmonium in the glimpse of the human face at the center of God's Love. And finally, it's on to the poetry of several American poets in the Catholic tradition, including Denise Levertov, Franz Wright, Scott Cairns, and Mary Karr, as well as poems by Robert Hayden, Lucille Clifton, Anne Sexton, Yeats, William Carlos Williams, and Wallace Stevens.

Undoubtedly there are many other voices that might be included in such a course: Augustine's *Confessions*, *Beowulf*, Langland, Caedmon, Chaucer, Chidiock Tichborn, Shakespeare, Catherine of Siena, the Metaphysical poets, including Donne and Herbert, then Dryden and Pope, Dostoevsky's *Crime and Punishment* and *The Brothers Karamazov*, Ernest Dowson, Paul Claudel, Charles Péguy, Jacques Maritain, Georges Bernanos, Pascal's *Pensées*, Joseph Conrad's *Heart of Darkness*, Graham Greene's *The Power and the Glory*, Walter Miller's *A Canticle for Leibowitz*, Ron Hansen's *Mariette in Ecstasy* and *Exiles*, Annie Dillard's *Pilgrim at Tinker Creek*, Patricia Hampl's *Virgin Time*, Alice McDermott's *Charming Billy*, the novels of Shusaku Endo, Francis Thompson's "The Hound of Heaven," Christina Rossetti, Oscar Wilde's *The Ballad of Reading Gaol*, David Jones, Les Murray, Geoffrey Hill, and Walker Percy. The feast is almost overwhelming in its breadth and depths, with a variety and versatility of voices that staggers the mind.

There's undoubtedly a rich heritage in the Catholic literary imagination, not only in the sense of a call for social justice, but also in terms of a particular understanding of the sacramental vision of the world: the fact of the Incarnation and what that means for our understanding of beauty and peace and understanding in the world. Or, as Flannery O'Connor writes in "A Good Man Is Hard to Find" as the family who will die that very day leaves their home in rural Georgia, only the narrator seems to notice that the trees themselves "were full of silver-white sunlight and the meanest of them sparkled." And if the meanest of the trees sparkle, so, too, does the criminal called the Misfit reveal a sparkle of goodness before he kills the grandmother, who reaches out to him, in the midst of her agony recognizing that he too is one of her children.

"If you came this way," T. S. Eliot tells us in the last of his *Four Quartets*,

Taking the route you would be likely to take
From the place you would be likely to come from . . .
If you came at night like a broken king,
If you came by day not knowing what you came for,
It would be the same, when you leave the rough road
And turn behind the pig-sty to the dull facade
And the tombstone. And what you thought you came for
Is only a shell, a husk of meaning
From which the purpose breaks only when it is fulfilled
If at all.[87]

So, too, Hopkins, at the close of "The Windhover," invites us to glimpse with him the majestic hawk buckle and plunge to the earth, like the God-man Christ buckling on the cross in the final sacrifice of himself for others. For only in the breaking of oneself does the fire flame out like shining from shook foil, or the kingfisher catch fire, or the dragonfly draw flame.

What the Catholic sacramental perspective teaches us is that the meanest thing carries within it something of inestimable worth, an inscape that gives to that particular thing a deeper value, which we are invited to discover and—when that value has been discovered—to offer our praise to the Giver. Francis and Ignatius acknowledged as much, as did Hopkins and O'Connor and Walker Percy and Ron Hansen and so many others.

Catholicism carries with it an inexhaustibly rich tradition, one shaped by two thousand years in which the imagination has been shaped by— and in turn has helped shape—Christianity, and, by extension, other cultures as we have come not only to *know* the Mystery but to *inhabit* it as well. In truth it has informed, reformed, and transformed what we read and see and understand about the entire spectrum of humanity. For if, as Hopkins said, the world is charged with the grandeur of God, so too is the Catholic imagination, with its emphasis on a God-saturated, God-centered world with its long tradition of sacramental beauty. There it is, then: the Catholic literary imagination, with each individual contribution to it like a tessera contributing to the larger edifice that has housed and still houses the Mystery, where a living voice still speaks, and where the Word still dwells as real presence.

Così la mente mia, tutta sospesa, Dante reports back to us in the final lines of the *Paradiso,* having finally gazed on the face of the Divine, *mirava fissa, immobile e attenta, / e sempre di mirar faceasi accesa.* A glimpse, then, into the Eternal that the pilgrim, after a lifetime's searching, seems finally to have been granted:

> So was my mind—completely rapt, intent,
> steadfast, and motionless—gazing; and it
> grew ever more enkindled as it watched.
>
> Whoever sees that Light is soon made such
> that it would be impossible for him
> to set that Light aside for other sight. . . .
>
> What little I recall is to be told,
> from this point on, in words more weak than those
> of one whose infant tongue still bathes at the breast. . . .[88]

What he sees, as he gazes into the Mystery, is the Three-in-One, the Godhead, the Trinity: three circles, each a different prismatic color, but all partaking in the whiteness of the Eternal Godhead, and that he now addresses:

> Eternal Light, You only dwell within
> Yourself, and only You know You; Self-knowing,
> Self-known, You love and smile upon Yourself!

That circle—which, begotten so, appeared
in You as light reflected—when my eyes
had watched it with attention for some time,

within itself and colored like itself,
to me seemed painted with our effigy,
so that my sight was set on it completely. . . .

I wished to see
the way in which our human effigy
suited the circle and found place in it—

and my own wings were far too weak for that.
But then my mind was struck by light that flashed
and, with this light, received what it had asked.

Here force failed my high fantasy; but my
desire and will were moved already—like
a wheel revolving uniformly—by
the Love that moves the sun and the other stars.[89]

A lifetime's searching by the Catholic imagination might be found
in these stirring lines that come at the close of Dante's epic, *The Divine
Comedy*. Wouldn't it be a gift to be able to offer that radiant tradition
a place at the table, and to join, ourselves, in sharing the fruits of this
feast?

15

"WHO IS THAT ON THE OTHER SIDE OF YOU?"

There's a moment in *The Waste Land* that has stayed with me for over fifty years now. It's a dreamlike moment in a dreamlike poem, where what is real and what is fiction flickers in the corner of one's sight. The passage occurs in the last section of the poem Eliot composed while recovering from a nervous breakdown in an asylum in Geneva, Switzerland, in the winter of 1921–22. A father recently dead—"those are pearls that were his eyes"—and the poet's marriage to the vivacious, unstable Vivien on the rocks, his search for something substantial or even consubstantial to shore up the splintering fragments of contemporary civilization, all these the poem records. But there's something more: the poet's thirst for life-giving water.

"If there were water," Eliot's indeterminate ghost-self sighs,

If there were water
And no rock
If there were rock
And also water
And water

A spring
A pool among the rock
If there were the sound of water only
Not the cicada
And dry grass singing
But sound of water over a rock
Where the hermit-thrush sings in the pine trees. . . .[90]

This is where he finds himself now, in the arid wasteland of the self, where "there is no water." Only desert, and a cold one at that, and the fevered mind, moving to and fro between two worlds, hallucinating. The passage, Eliot tells us in one of his famous footnotes, was "stimulated by the account of one of the Antarctic expeditions."[91] One of Shackleton's, he thinks. As Eliot recollects it, "the party of explorers, at the extremity of their strength, had the constant delusion that there was one more member than could actually be counted."[92]

The source is indeed Sir Ernest Shackleton, whose memoir of the polar expedition undertaken at the height of World War I recounts a grueling march "of 36 hours over the unnamed mountains and glaciers of South Georgia," when it seemed to him "that we were four, not three."[93] Here is how Eliot reconfigures that scene in the final section of *The Waste Land*, cutting the number of travelers from three to two, expanded inexplicably by the hooded stranger at their side:

Who is the third who walks always beside you?
When I count, there are only you and I together
But when I look ahead up the white road
There is always another one walking beside you
Gliding wrapt in a brown mantle, hooded
I do not know whether a man or a woman
—But who is that on the other side of you?[94]

Anyone who has read Luke's Gospel knows what this passage echoes, as undoubtedly it was meant to do: the scene that takes place on that first Easter Sunday, when two of Christ's defeated disciples are on the road to a village some seven miles from Jerusalem. "They were talking with each other about everything that had happened," Luke tells us— the surprise capture of Jesus in the garden, his rushed trial, followed by his crucifixion outside the city walls (see Lk. 24:13–35). The Jewish and Roman authorities had done away with this troublesome, charismatic leader, leaving his disciples to scatter like shot dogs.

Then, suddenly, while they are discussing these catastrophic events, Jesus is present among them, the two of them three now, though—as Luke tells us—the disciples "were kept from recognizing him." And, in a remarkable moment in the narrative retelling of this account, this unrecognized figure asks them what it is they have been discussing. "They stood still," Luke says, "their faces downcast. One of them, named Cleopas, asked him, 'Are you only a visitor to Jerusalem and do not know the things that have happened there in these days?'"

"What things?" the figure asks.

"About Jesus of Nazareth," they reply, and proceed to tell him of the last few days—"we had hoped that he was the one who was going to redeem Israel," not leaving out how the women had gone to the tomb and found it empty.

The unrecognized Jesus listens, then chides them for not taking to heart the words of the prophets who went before: "Did not the Christ have to suffer these things and then enter his glory?" Then, Luke tells us, he went on to explain to them "what was said in all the Scriptures concerning himself."

At that point, with darkness coming on, the figure agrees to stay with the two at their invitation, and Luke's narrative continues:

When he was at the table with them, he took bread, gave thanks, broke it and began to give it to them. Then their eyes were opened, and they

recognized him, and he disappeared from their sight. . . . They got up
and returned at once to Jerusalem. There they found the Eleven and . . .
Then the two [who had first encountered Jesus on the road] told what had
happened on the way, and how Jesus was recognized by them when he
broke the bread.[95]

In the breaking of the bread: Luke's passage always stirs me, because it
contains in outline the essentials of the Mass. "And beginning with
Moses and all the Prophets," Luke wrote, "Jesus explained to them what
was said in all the Scriptures concerning himself." There we have the
first part of the Mass: readings from the Old and New Testament and
the Psalms, followed in turn by words of encouragement, and then the
incredible gift of the breaking of the bread, as Christ's very self—his
body and his blood—is shared by the entire faith community.

For me, as for others—from Robert Southwell and Gerard Manley
Hopkins to G. K. Chesterton and David Jones to Eliot himself and
Robert Lowell and John Berryman and Denise Levertov and Ron Hansen
and Franz Wright and Mary Karr and Marie Howe—this story of the
one who walks beside us has been at the center of what we believe,
and why we write as we do. It is the core, the central brotherhood and
sisterhood, if you will, the lens of companionship. *Com pan*. The word
at its root means those with whom we would share our bread, which
includes, finally, whoever approaches the table.

There are really two activities that I can point to over a lifetime
of teaching and writing, and both are intertwined: the word and that
toward which the word aims, the deeper reality within appearances.
Or, as Hopkins called it, the inscape of things. Call it the sacramental
aspect of things, the sense that the Mystery hovers over and within
everything, illumines and shines through them. Or call it real presence,
in and beyond the transformation in the Mass, which points to how
Christ plays—as Hopkins puts it—in "ten thousand faces not his." Or,
as Jewish tradition has it, a hundred blessings a day to count.

Points of light, grace notes, luminations, epiphanies, poetic insights. Call them what you will. Love embodied, in and through the Creation and, yes, our very lives.

16
THE CRY OF THE POOR

I should have known when I signed on at Boston College, and joined my efforts to a project like the university's "Roundtable Focusing On the Advancing of the Mission of Catholic Higher Education," that at some point I would find an elephant crashing around the room and—as Flannery O'Connor famously said of Christ—throwing everything off balance. What I didn't see was that the unassuming Sister Amata Miller, one of the invited guests to the BC Roundtable, would be the one who brought that necessary raging presence through the hall doors and into the room where we met. In fact, I found that elephant to be breathing heavily down my neck as we reached, somewhat unsteadily, the closing sessions of those discussions.

When I first addressed this gathering at its outset, and spoke on the subject of the great Catholic literary tradition—alluding to Dante, Donne, Herbert, Milton, Hopkins, Chesterton, Eliot, Merton, and Flannery O'Connor, among others—and then went on to speak of the problem of evil in a literary context—the purgatorial journey, those glitter-go shards of grasshopper flights into the transcendent we may be blessed with—I had not taken into sufficient account how uncomfortable I found it then, and find it now, to look daily into the broken face of Christ as it manifests itself in the poor, the trapped, the sick, the hungry, and the homeless. Having myself been born into a world that inhabited the lower end of the economic food chain, it was natural to want to escape that and, by grace of faith, the luck of being born into a barely post-Depression America, where it was possible for millions to make a good living and—given an education—to find a way out of the worst aspects of marginal poverty. How much more pleasant, really, to be able to dwell in Dante's Circle of Philosophers, where one could discourse on beauty and truth and the possible existence of God, or muse endlessly with Li Po, Proust, Rilke, and Wallace Stevens on Plato's worlds of shadow and light over an exquisite glass or three of chardonnay.

And then to have all of that upturned as one enters a subway station somewhere in Brooklyn and—like that young Jesuit priest in the 1973 film *The Exorcist*—to find some bum, some homeless person lying against one of the steel support columns in his own stale urine, shaming you into handing over whatever spare change—"make that a buck, pal"— you have. Or St. Francis, confronting and then embracing a full-blown leper on the outskirts of Assisi. Or Nathanael Hawthorne, walking down the corridors of a British orphanage in Liverpool during his time as US representative in the mid-1850s and seeing a little boy, his nose running, beseeching him with liquid eyes to pick him up and embrace him, if only for a moment.

Nathanael Hawthorne: father of Rose Hawthorne, who would go on to become the founder of an order of sisters whose special charism was to care for the cancer-ridden. Or Dr. William Carlos Williams, on a house call to a poor old widow living alone, examining her and making her comfortable in the sharp winter cold, and then walking down into the basement, taking off his jacket and rolling up his sleeves, and getting a fire going in the coal furnace. For what good would it have been, he says, to merely wish her well and leave her to the cold before moving on to his next house call?

Sister Amata Miller of the Immaculate Heart of Mary, professor of economics with a doctorate from Berkeley, and director of the Myser Initiative on Catholic Identity at St. Catherine University, has spent most of her life thinking about, championing, and working with the poor in one capacity or another, always as an advocate for our neediest sisters and brothers. For the common wealth, she has insisted now for over half a century, *must be* distributed in a just and equitable manner.

Helping those she has taught over the years become agents of social justice has been part of her work. And Michigan Supreme Court justice Maura Corrigan, her student back in the volatile 1960s, has said that Sister Amata had the most profound influence on her of any teacher in her life. "She opened worlds of knowledge to us and offered a firm commitment to scholarship and rationality in this often-chaotic world"—a gift offered generously in this often-chaotic world.[96]

Perhaps because I'm a slow learner, I had to read and reread the talk she delivered among us over and over before I began to plumb the complexities of her arguments for distributive economic justice and an end to obscene poverty in a period of unprecedented affluence.[97] She outlined for us the roots of economic parity and social responsibility with its roots in those Jewish agricultural societies we find in Exodus, Deuteronomy, Leviticus, Isaiah, and Amos. She underlined, too, God's determination to free his people from slavery in Egypt, and the Jubilee Year, which called for the return of all lands to their original owners without compensation every fifty years, as well as of sabbaticals, by which slaves and debtors and the very soil itself might be freed every seventh year. She has spoken of interest-free loans for the poor, and of the radical economics Jesus himself practiced, where wealth was shared and where we were responsible for the care and well-being of one another.

Here, she has called upon modern Catholic social teaching to guide us in bringing a moral dimension into public discussions of social issues.

In short, she has invited us to consider what happens to the economy, a machine that should hum along quietly to take care of the needs of all of us, when it malfunctions. Doesn't it keep most human beings not only from flourishing as they should, stripping us of our inherent dignity, while money pools lifelessly like blood oil around the Gucci shoes of a relative handful? And then, as she concluded in this address, she reminded us that we who teach and work at Christian colleges and universities must play a key role in fostering that necessary political will in our students that will make them more fully aware of our shared social responsibility.

She reminded us, too, of the mission statements of our Catholic universities and colleges, and of our promise to educate the whole person through the study of the liberal arts—theology, philosophy, history, literature—all rooted in the Catholic intellectual tradition. But she also reminded us that too often the economic dimension of life has been ignored as something to be taught only in business classes, so that we, uninformed about the economic dimensions of reality, too often seek instead dreamy myths that tend to evaporate in due course, leaving us all the worse for it. Rightfully so, she spoke of our contact with the poor and marginalized, including those we meet or pass by every day of our lives, giving to money and wealth "a false dominance" by accepting the inequities and exclusions that go with a rigged market economy. Our rich heritage of Catholic social teaching, she reminded us, must be integrated into our general education core, and it is our responsibility as teachers to make clear to our students what their rights and responsibilities as human beings are, and do this by our actions rather than by merely using words.

I think of my own Jesuit son working to feed the hungry in Mexico, or working with L'Arche communities in Seattle, or working with the Chinese population in San Jose. Or my wife, Eileen, working with the poor in western Massachusetts or in the backwoods of Kentucky. Or our son John, who worked with Mexican street gangs in Tucson as part of his assignment with the Jesuit Volunteer Corps, a year that determined that he would work with the too-often, neglected schoolchildren of Manchester, Connecticut. Or our son Mark, who works with a large number of Korean and Mexican boys in grades six through nine and who—in spite of coming from wealth—are sent to schools far from their homes for months at a time and who crave parental guidance and personal attention. When I see such examples, I cannot help but think that if I could only hang on to the hem of my family's coats, I too might make it through the gates someday.

The cry of the poor, calling out to the world. You must change your life, Rilke tells us, before you dare to speak to others, especially in poems. You must feed Christ's sheep if you would truly love him. Then multiply such instances, such Christlike instances, by a hundred-, a thousand-, a millionfold, and one begins to see how real change could come about in our world.

You do what you can, remembering that one feeds the hungry not only with bread, but with words and by acts of attention to each person one teaches, if that is the charism one has been given. For in truth, one serves the hungry not only by offering them bread and fish, but also by teaching them how to farm and fish so that they can in turn feed themselves and others.

Of course, if you are truly fortunate, you might offer them the bread of Christ on a Sunday morning in an old mill town. And, as they receive the precious bread one by one by one—the young, the teenagers, the middle-aged, the elderly—you feel a joy you cannot contain, until you are fighting back tears as the hungry are fed, and you, too, are fed by their presence. And you understand then that it is just as Christ said, that there is a oneness beyond language, all of it wrapped in a shawl of light because we who are poor, along with our neighbors, near and far, have been so richly fed.

17
IN THE FOOTSTEPS OF IGNATIUS

After an awful night's flight from Boston to Madrid, during which dozens of teenagers roamed the airplane aisles shouting and joking in Spanish, my wife, Eileen, and I land, and we're greeted by a representative of Washington Theological Union, the sponsor of our retreat. Professor Ed McCormack has, for the past twenty years, offered retreats based on the *Spiritual Exercises* for high school and college students. Like our other retreat leaders, he has been preparing for this journey for a long time.

So begins an eight-day trip through Spain's Basque country in the footsteps of St. Ignatius Loyola, the sixteenth-century founder of the Jesuits. There are twenty-six of us, divided evenly between men and women: six couples, five priests, several single women, and some half dozen others who are all taking the trip as the culmination of a course in the *Spiritual Exercises* under the guidance of Professor McCormack and Joan Knetemann, director of the department of institutional advancement at this graduate school.

As with any pilgrims, in any era, we all have our own reasons for being here. Some are more civilized than others, but among the spread is an interest in history and culture, a devotion to prayer, a love of good tapas and Spanish wine, and a generous dose of curiosity. Then there's the deeper reason, unarticulated but necessary, that is seldom clear to any of us until we have made the journey and that may not show itself for weeks or even months or years afterward.

With cameras and journals we hit the ground recording what seems obvious by its grandeur or its hints of the sublime: the grand edifices of Madrid, the medieval splendors of Burgos, St. Francis Xavier's fortresslike dwelling, and the marble and stone piles of the Sanctuary of St. Ignatius in Loyola, enfolded within the apparently fortified structure where Ignatius grew up, the building itself now enclosed within a great baroque church.

Accommodations range from the modest, comfortable meals and dorm rooms at Centro Arrupe to a sumptuous dinner and a room at the Parador in Cardona. There are tapas bars in Pamplona that are, as they say, to die for, together with an ascetic-looking guide there who speaks of his distaste for Hemingway with his incessant talking of the running of the bulls. So wrapped up is our guide in these canned remarks that we barely notice the sidewalk plaque with embossed chain links and the familiar IHS at the top, followed by the words: *Aquí Cayó Herido San Ignacio de Loyola 20 de Mayo de 1521 A.M.D.G.* (Here St. Ignatius Loyola fell wounded on May 20, 1521): on that day, a French cannonball ricocheted off a stone wall and struck Ignatius, shattering both his legs, so that the fortress he was protecting against an overwhelming French enemy had to be surrendered because no one else was willing to carry on the fight besides this crazy Basque.

In San Sebastián, we peer down at the coastal waters from above the striated rocks, and it is as if the wind itself had carved these lines into the hillside. The image of a sixteenth-century double-masted ship, uncovered on one of the walls in Loyola's house, is a reminder of his family's connection to the sea.

From miles away, as we travel south, the serrated edges of Montserrat are visible, and nearby Manresa, where Ignatius lived in a cave for a year. There, amid the now-baroque splendors of the little chapel, I touch the cold exposed rock he must have touched, and I realize that in terms of geological formation a mere moment separates me from the man who lived and shaped the *Spiritual Exercises* that have, over the years and decades, shaped my wife, my sons, and myself.

In Barcelona we discover Antoni Gaudí's magnificent Sagrada Familia Basilica, begun in 1882 and still unfinished. The architect died in 1926, but work on this neo-Gothic, Art Nouveau edifice is expected to go on into the late 2020s. It's breathtaking, really, even sublime, and it captures in its magnitude something of Barcelona's audacious spirit. George Orwell called this incarnation of Catalonian Modernism one of the most hideous buildings in the world. To some it is a Spanish Disneyland. But to others it is the masterwork of one of the most original architects of the last two centuries.

Several priests in our group concelebrate Mass in the crypt of Barcelona's cathedral, dedicated to St. Eulalia, martyred at thirteen in the fourth century. Afterward, I stare into the marble faces of the indifferent Roman authorities surrounding her sepulcher, then into the faces of her torturers. After several attempts to kill her failed, on February 12, 303, she was stripped and crucified. But a heavy snow fell and covered her nakedness. As a sign, legend has it, never once has it snowed in Barcelona on that day.

I grew up with legends like these, at which in truth the modern mind balks. Yet no matter how many times Eulalia's story has been replayed, the pride and stupidity that violated her youthful innocence end up with her torturers damning themselves, as the faces of stupidity and hatred are held up to the flickering candlelight in the crypt beside this young girl, who has set her eyes on something many refuse to see. "We had the experience but missed the meaning," Eliot wrote as he approached his own omega point in life. He for one saw that the "approach to the meaning restores the experience / In a different form, beyond any meaning / We can assign to happiness."[98]

I remember a time, when I was half my present age—*nel mezzo del cammin di nostra vita*—driving a rented car through the Tuscan hills with Eileen beside me and Allen Mandelbaum, my mentor and renowned Dante translator, with his partner, trying to relax in the back seat. The roads zigzagged through ancient towns as stone buildings loomed up on either side, until Eileen became ill with motion sickness to the point that I had to pull over. That's where Allen spotted a lead pipe channeling cold mountain water. He covered her forehead with a handkerchief soaked in those refreshing waters, while I paced back and forth, eager to push on to the next church with its murals and paintings.

Now, thirty-five years later, with the news that my cherished teacher and friend has died, I realize what the heart of this pilgrimage in the footsteps of Ignatius comes down to, as an experience is replayed for me with a clarity that haunts and astounds.

One morning on our bus trip, we found ourselves riding up the precipitous mountain road that clings to the edge of the Aiskorri Range, en route to the Franciscan sanctuary of Our Lady at Aránzazu in the Basque country of Oñati. There's a shrine to the Virgin at the summit, on the site where Mary is believed to have appeared to a shepherd a generation before Ignatius was born. The shepherd said he saw Mary among the thorn bushes and exclaimed, "Arantzan zu?!" (Is that you, among the thorns?). Linguistically, it's true, the phrase means simply "place of the hawthorns." But now the rugged mountain landscape itself announces our arrival at the Franciscan sanctuary of Our Lady of Aránzazu. The bus swerves back and forth, yawing over the indifferent crevasses below.

Eileen, thank God, recovered in time. Where she sat she had a view of the hillside and had taken her Dramamine. But just behind us, on the other side of the bus, one of our group, nauseous from motion sickness, began to vomit. There was a clamor to the young Peruvian bus driver to get the bus off the narrow, winding road as soon as possible. And then our fellow pilgrim, stricken, wobbled down the rear steps of the bus with the help of Joan and some others. I watched him, as if this were some movie: an old man—like myself—dizzy and helpless. Then, suddenly I, too, found myself descending quickly down those same steps, daring myself to do what I was about to do, as I began wiping the vomit from his shirt and pants, comforting him as I could.

I later remember looking into his eyes, which had grown suddenly deep, to see . . . what? The eyes of Ignatius and Francis of Assisi and the eyes of Eulalia, and then, yes, Christ's eyes looking back at me. Soon, with cars speeding past us in both directions, Joan asked me to get back on the bus where it was safer. But an odd sense of peace had come over me as I sat down beside my wife. Then it came to me, as it has to so many other pilgrims, that this is why I had come all these thousands of miles: to find Christ here, now, at this junction, even as I learned to find myself.

CAN ONE STILL WRITE A
CHRIST-CENTERED POETRY?

S ome thirty years ago I was asked by a literary magazine to take part in a discussion on the topic of Christian poetry in our time. Here's the way the topic arose. One of the editors of the magazine had recently given a reading at a large university. At the dinner party after the reading, he wanted to recommend a book by a poet whose name he'd momentarily forgotten. "He's a fine poet," the editor said, trying to describe the man. Someone, he said, who'd recently moved to the Midwest to teach. "A Christian poet."

And suddenly there was laughter around the table. A *Christian* poet? Well, if he was a Christian poet, someone offered, perhaps he wrote verse for Hallmark. More laughter. The editor returned to his meal, smarting. Then he remembered the poet's name: Scott Cairns. The name rang a bell. Several at the table had read his work and liked it. "Oh," someone said, "he's not a Christian poet. He's a poet who sometimes writes about religion."

What was happening here? If the poet under discussion had been Dante or Hopkins, the editor wondered, would the tone at that table have been different? What was it about the idea of someone writing poetry from the Christian perspective today that he or she should be met with derision, suspicion, disbelief, even contempt?

And so, the editors of the magazine decided to ask Cairns himself about this reaction to the very idea of the Christian poet.

It was a huge question, Cairns began, and even to begin to answer it would mean looking at the complex array of recent cultural history. It would also mean having the feedback of a number of poets for whom Christianity was still a viable option. In short: a unique and valuable way of speaking to others. First of all, he began, the current climate in which an audience could actually laugh at the idea of a modern Christian voice was not "necessarily the fault of the secular reader." After all, the history of twentieth-century American Christianity—its most vocal elements, anyway—had been "a largely anti-intellectual endeavor, largely suspicious of art in general, and pretty much dumbed down in comparison to earlier epochs," making what had passed for Christian poetry look like "pretty thin soup."

I think Scott got it right there. Poetry—good poetry, at least—is hard enough to write as it is. And the best poetry, the poetry taught in our colleges and universities, is for the most part a product of the secular imagination in what has been dubbed a post-Christian era. Consider the American (and British and Irish) poets who are regularly taught in our modern and contemporary poetry courses: Yeats, Frost, Stevens, Williams, Eliot, Pound, Marianne Moore, Wilfred Owen, Hart Crane, Langston Hughes, W. H. Auden, and Dylan Thomas among the moderns, then Roethke, Bishop, Berryman, Lowell, Sylvia Plath, and Anne Sexton among the middle generation, then Ginsberg, James Wright, Frank O'Hara, Robert Creeley, Gary Snyder, John Ashbery, Philip Levine, Gerald Stern, Denise Levertov, Sharon Olds, Charles Simic, Charles Wright, Yusef Komunyakaa, Audre Lorde, Billy Collins. Add to this, of course, the new voices constantly being added to the mix, and throw in your own favorite half dozen, and voilà! There you have it.

Note that I've privileged the structure of the university here, as if the general reader of poetry had all but disappeared. And yet the truth is— at least in my experience—that the general reader of poetry *has* all but disappeared. Of course, the reasons for this also need to be explored. It may well be that Modernism—a poem, say, like T. S. Eliot's *The Waste Land*—took the poem out of general circulation as early as the 1920s and sent it to the classroom, where it could be analyzed and understood, but only with the help of the professor and an armamentarium of secondary sources. Certainly, William Carlos Williams believed this to be the case. And in the 1930s and 1940s there were any number of poet-critics who were also academics—figures like Allen Tate, Robert Penn Warren, John Crowe Ransom, Stephen Spender, and Mark Van Doren—who made of the New Criticism, with its multivalent, complex readings of the text, a significant industry of reading poetry.

Because so many American poets have been affiliated with one university or the other for the past sixty years, it is no wonder that this has continued. In the 1950s Allen Ginsberg and the Beats forcibly wrenched the poem from the university and were immensely successful, at least for a while. But even Robert Creeley and Charles Olsen returned to the classroom, and Ginsberg was often seen reading or lecturing in a university setting.

The truth is that it's almost always easier for a poet to talk about anything, or nothing, so long as the tone is engaging, witty, and avoids— as the old saw goes—certain kinds of politics, usually of a conservative cast, or religion, unless it be of a New Age or vaguely Eastern kind. In fact, it's far more acceptable in the contemporary poem to use an openly blasphemous frame of mind than to approach the mystery at the heart of Christianity in anything like a serious frame of mind. One can mock Christianity without reproach, or approach the poem from the frame of mind that shows you've escaped the ravages of faith, but it will be much harder to speak from the perspective of someone drawn to the Mystery of the presence—that is, to the sacramental "real."

By "serious" I do not mean somber or poetry without a sense of humor or serious play; that element, I think, is necessary for any poem to work. But the widespread presumption is that the Christian poet by his or her very nature has some design on you, other than that of writing a poem that taught the poet—and therefore the reader—something he or she had no other way of understanding until the actual writing of the poem itself revealed it.

A passage in Flannery O'Connor's "The River" speaks to this very issue. A young boy named Harry, some four or five years old, has been brought down to a river by his zealous babysitter to hear the Reverend Bevel Summers preach on a Sunday morning and, as events turn out, to be baptized by the preacher in that same sun-glinting, red-muddy river, and to pray for the boy's mother, who is ill—the boy tells the preacher—with a hangover. There's something comic about the whole scene and about the way O'Connor presents it. A nineteen-year-old preacher in rolled-up khaki trousers, standing ten feet out in the river. He's nondescript, really: tall, thin, with "light-colored hair . . . cut in sideburns that curved into the hollows of his cheeks. His face was all bone and red light reflected from the river. . . . He was singing in a high twangy voice, above the singing on the bank, and he kept his hands behind him and his head tilted back."[99] A rube, we think, a country hick, about whom Mr. Paradise—the man with the tumor over his ear who mocks the whole scene, but keeps coming back, despite himself, to witness it—shouts to the crowd: "Pass the hat and give this kid his money. That's what he's here for."[100]

But there's no mocking what the preacher has to say. His voice "grew soft and musical," O'Connor writes, as he proclaims the message to this group of hillbillies and misfits, the poor and the powerless, like the woman who has brought the boy here to be baptized, a woman with a husband in the hospital and on permanent disability who works the nightshift and weekends to keep three sullen boys and a teenage girl fed and housed. "Listen to what I got to say, you people!" this modern John the Baptist says. Christ is the River of Life and the River of Love, he says, and the muddy red river symbolizes the red river of Jesus's blood.

And then the sheer, mesmerizing poetry of the preacher's witness, a riff off the vision of Ezekiel, who sang of seeing the river flowing eastward from the temple itself, growing larger and deeper, and teeming with life:

> All the rivers come from that one River and go back to it like it was the
> ocean sea and if you believe, you can lay your pain in that River and get
> rid of it because that's the River that was made to carry sin. It's a river
> full of pain itself, pain itself, moving toward the Kingdom of Christ, to
> be washed away, slow, you people, slow as this here old red water river
> round my feet.[101]

Let this episode serve as parable for the problems involved in our time in getting poetry of a sacramental order a viable hearing: a Catholic writer writing about a hillbilly preacher who promises nothing, really, except what one could bring to the river, the river of faith, speaking in a language that echoes the prophets and John the Baptist. I suppose it is why I find myself returning so often to O'Connor, who in her short life managed to capture the complex dualities and contradictions inherent in our world, one caught in the ironies and slipperiness of our language, to say nothing of our inability (or refusal) to pay attention to the other.

When I was poetry editor of *America*, I received well over a thousand poetry submissions a year, even though I could publish only twelve of those, and one of those was for a monetary prize. I got to see a lot of well-meaning poems, many by ministers and clergy and religious, among others, with the ages of those submitting ranging from students in junior high to the octogenarian. Often as not there was a well-developed religious sensibility present in the poetry, but the poetry itself was lacking. Not the verse forms, for often those were present. What was missing was the thing that makes the poem live not only as a poem, but as a felt expression of a religious sensibility, where the spiritual dimension and the words come together into a surprising and harmonious whole.

Of course, that's true in part because good poetry is hard enough to come by. But then to find this other quality, this further dimension:

that's far rarer still. Perhaps that is as it should be. This is not the age of Dante, a poet who could rely on the Scholastic synthesis formulated by Aquinas, who brought together not only the best of Aristotelian thought but also patristics and those brilliant "outsiders," Maimonides and Averroes—in short, a synthesis of classical, Jewish, Muslim, and Christian thought. Nor is this a Metaphysical age, which generated poets like Donne, Herbert, Crashaw, and Vaughan.

We must start—as always in the case of poetry—with the poem itself. Apart from Hopkins, and to a lesser degree Eliot and Jones and W. H. Auden, poetry has to consider the brilliant work of writers for whom the various formulations of Judaism and Christianity were problematic at best, for in truth Christianity for Yeats and Frost and Pound and Stevens and Williams and Hart Crane was something to be plundered. Something that acted as an irritant of sorts. Something to be used where its stories or symbols could be employed in building a new temple, if you will.

Harold Bloom speaks of the Paterian aesthetic, often crossed with the naysaying of a Nietzsche. Cross those figures with the Romantic tradition—Blake and Shelley, Wordsworth, Coleridge, and Keats, and in some instances even the cool comic detachment of a Byron—and you come up with a fascinating potpourri of influences.

I mention these sources because when I come upon William Carlos Williams or Robert Lowell—or even Emily Dickinson—invoking the Blessed Mother, I look twice to see with what tone they were invoking. And what of the case of Wallace Stevens speaking of the hero in his time in terms that all but name the presence of Christ?

Still, it's a strategy, this indirect darting, this almost subliminal invocation that vanishes even as you try to fix it, which may in fact be one of the most successful poetic strategies of our time. I have called it—in another context—a kind of grasshopper transcendency: the momentary lift or epiphany or spot of time, in which something is for a moment glimpsed, like subatomic motes, if you will, before it disappears. It is as much a question of the shifts in syntax, or the ambiguous modifier or pronoun or the poem ending with a question rather than a statement that allows for these luminous fulgurations, these brief glimpses in and out of time. Wallace Stevens is a good example of the sort of thing I'm talking about here. Take a late poem from *Transport to Summer*, a poem with the arresting title "The Good Man Has No Shape," and watch as Stevens fills in the image of Jesus of Nazareth between the lines, without ever naming him:

> Through centuries he lived in poverty,
> God only was his only elegance.
>
> Then generation by generation he grew
> Stronger and freer, a little better off.
>
> He lived each life because, if it was bad,
> He said a good life would be possible.
>
> At last the good life came, good sleep, bright fruit,
> And Lazarus betrayed him to the rest,
>
> Who killed him, sticking feathers in his flesh
> To mock him. They placed with him in his grave
>
> Sour wine to warm him, an empty book to read,
> And over it they set a jagged sign,
>
> Epitaphium to his death, which read,
> The Good Man Has No Shape, as if they knew.[102]

Here, in fourteen lines made up of seven unrhymed couplets, Stevens has re-created a mythology of Jesus as the essential good man, a mythology in which such a one is killed by being stuck with feathers as a mockery of his divinity. Even Lazarus betrays Jesus in Stevens's retelling, because Jesus raised Lazarus from the tomb—or so Lazarus reports in this retelling. And this is something that the authorities, as in John's Gospel, cannot allow. In Stevens's retelling, Jesus preached the good life, which for Stevens consists of "good sleep" and "bright fruit." But Jesus also promises that even if one's life turns out badly, there remains the possibility that things might be different. After the mob kills Jesus they place the sign not above his head on the cross, but over his grave. Finally, Stevens rewrites the sign above Jesus's head. Not *Jesus of Nazareth, King of the Jews,* now, the sign placed there by the Roman authorities to mock not only Jesus but the Jewish people in general, but rather the general taunt against humanity itself that indeed *The Good Man Has No Shape.* The Good Man, in other words is and must remain an ideal, a fabrication, a lie, the underlying reading being that there never has been any such thing as a Good Man. And then, just as you think the poem is over, Stevens destabilizes everything he has said by adding the closing qualifier, "as if they knew."

Stevens's linguistic strategy speaks to an age given to ambivalence and uncertainty. As he grew older, he tended to hover somewhere in between, with an "and yet . . . and yet . . . and yet," or an "as if," which made every certainty that followed that "as if" conditioned upon it, like a lawyer inserting qualifications and exceptions in a contract that could look as if it were offering us the world, even as it left us, finally, empty-handed of everything but a glittering promise. The sort of thing we get every day, really, in ads that are sent in our general direction, and that seem to promise those on either side of the belief equation something for their time and trouble.

Much modern and contemporary poetry, approaching the question of belief, follows this pattern, often substituting itself in place of that belief, not as an addition but as something like a momentarily satisfying aesthetic response, as if the poem were a self-enclosed artifact or urn, and the linguistic and formal resolution something to quiet the churning, dissatisfied mind. Or, as Stevens himself once put it, "Men feel that the imagination is the next greatest power to faith: the reigning prince."[103]

But which is the reigning prince? Faith? Or the Imagination? In either event, the question remains: is this enough to satisfy the soul? Is it?

EPILOGUE:
ON THE WORK STILL TO BE DONE

"Beauty will save the world."

—Fyodor Dostoevsky

Back in the summer of 1989, Greg Wolfe and Harold Fickett wrote me that they were starting up a new magazine to be called *Image: A Journal of the Arts and Religion,* and would I be interested in serving on the board and perhaps contributing something to the first issue? In truth, I had to rub my eyes a couple of times to be sure I was reading the letter correctly. Were these guys serious about starting a magazine that would be devoted to what the great twentieth-century theologian Hans Urs von Balthasar called Beauty—a serious magazine devoted to art, literature, faith, and mystery?

Could such a venue actually exist and flourish for more than a few issues, like so many of the "Little magazines" in the early part of the twentieth century? Could this magazine devote itself to what was central to me as well as others who had been deeply affected by writers like Hopkins, Eliot, Auden, Flannery O'Connor, Walker Percy, Thomas Merton, J. F. Powers, Seamus Heaney, as well as Lowell, Berryman, and Denise Levertov?

But what of my own generation and the generation coming up after me? What had we to contribute to the canon? Of one's own generation, one is always less certain because the votes aren't in yet. Nothing's settled, and the dust of the laborers still fills the air, complicating matters. Who could I turn to, talk with, learn from, and offer something of my own? I remember one of my colleagues at the University of Massachusetts, years ago, speaking only half-jokingly of the "invincible ignorance" of Catholics like myself—or of those Catholics with their "wafer god." One learned to laugh and swallow it all, joking along that being a Catholic or Christian intellectual was something of an oxymoron, but still it stung, which meant this: that you got up again and stumbled on.

In my own family there was nothing, outside of my Lutheran mother's yearning, like an intellectually sound faith community. There was Mass, the Rosary, the nights spent each month in Nocturnal Adoration, or serving as an altar boy in grade school, high school, and college, or my year in a Marianist school in Beacon, New York, preparing for the priesthood. In my New York City and Long Island neighborhoods you didn't talk literature unless you wanted to get punched in the mouth, and religion was a matter of being Catholic, Protestant, or Jew, as Will Herberg taught us to think.

College changed some of that. The Great Books courses from Homer and Virgil, the pre-Socratics and Plato and Aristotle, Sappho and Catullus, Suetonius and Livy, through Boethius and Aquinas and Duns Scotus, and on and on (happily) through the central Middle Ages and the Renaissance and Reformation and into the age of dark Enlightenment and on through the Romantics and Modernists and post-Modernists and. . . .

But as a writer who saw vast riches in the Psalms and Genesis and Exodus and Deuteronomy and the Gospels, and even the uncanonical texts and the church fathers (both East and West), and those other riches offered by the secular classics, I asked myself who was there to share this with, not merely as a professor but as a writer and as a believer.

No wonder then that *Image*, addressing itself as it did to art, religion, and beauty, was so important in reminding me that there was a viable and electric community out there committed to the same values I'd found essential to my own life: oases, if you will, in the vast deserts of secularism or the dumbing down that passed muster for so much of American culture. It's not something I can easily talk about, even with writers who are close to my heart but who don't share the same spiritual values, or see what I see, so that I find myself shifting constantly to some other idiom or topic—("How 'bout them Red Sox?" or "Weird weather we been havin', no?" or "Nice tie, where'd you get it, bro?").

And then one discovers someone like Greg Wolfe, who has managed to bring together such a remarkable collection of poets, fiction writers, and writers of the neglected Belles Lettres. Here are just a few of the names of those I've worked with or met or been privileged to learn from: Richard Wilbur, Annie Dillard, Kathleen Norris, Ron Hansen, Barry Moser, Bob Clarke, Patricia Hampl, Brett Lott, Luci Shaw, Louise Erdrich, Doris Betts, Reynolds Price, Chaim Potok, Anne Tyler, John Irving, Tobias and Catherine Wolff, Marilynne Robinson, Thomas Lynch, Franz Wright, Mary Karr, Andre Dubus the elder and the younger, Scott Cairns, Andrew Hudgins, Edward Hirsch, Philip Levine, Geoffrey Hill, Richard Rodriguez, Dana Gioia, Alice McDermott, Greg Orr, Brigit Pegeen Kelly, Angela Alaimo O'Donnell, Julia Kasdorf, Linford Detweiler, Karin Bergquist, Suzanne Wolfe, Leslie Leyland Fields, Marilyn Nelson, Mary Kenagy, Philip Kolin, Don Martin, and—really—so many more, including my "students," thanks to *Image*, many of whom have gone on to become seasoned and recognized writers.

Recently, I was asked to read a poet new to me, a woman steeped in the Christian tradition who had been published in *Image*, and provide an endorsement. I began browsing, then reading, then found myself mesmerized by what I read. In truth, reading her was like entering the dawn of the eighth day of creation, the poems were that beautiful and true. The self, the other, the dream: all seemed to merge here into one, as I felt reading Dante's vision of the Trinity, each utterance a distinctive selving radiant with love and utter caring. How was it, I found myself asking, that a poet today could so quickly and quietly and seamlessly draw me into the living dream of the Holy?

But there you have it. Something I have actually experienced a number of times when I was privileged to teach, lead, and more often than not, learn from writers Harold Fickett and Greg Wolfe brought together in Colorado or Santa Fe or Rigby Island off Puget Sound, lessons I brought back with me to the University of Massachusetts, Amherst, and later to Boston College or to the tufa cliffs of Orvieto, where—for a blessed month in April several years back—I followed in the footsteps of Scott Cairns to teach students from Gordon College and Wheaton and Calvin College.

Let me end by echoing what my friend Ron Hansen has said about Greg Wolfe: that he was "among the first to perceive . . . a renaissance of religious humanism in the arts: of writers and artists who did not abandon their faith in Mystery but drew courage, guidance, and inspiration from it." In fact, he has been—and continues to be—"one of the most incisive and persuasive voices of our generation."

Having been in the thick of much of what Greg has been doing and writing over the past twenty-five years, I have too often taken his advocacy for what matters most to so many of us for granted, as if things were proceeding normally, or the way they were supposed to in the ongoing work of bearing witness to the Mystery. But then a time comes when one stops long enough to consider what in fact has been done and continues to be done, and how Greg, in his daily work as in his epistles to the Oklahomans, Californians, New Mexicans, Georgians, Ohioans, New Yorkers, and even those from far-flung Massachusetts had transformed the way we see and value the Mystery by adding—as he has in his inimitable, beautifully dogged, and unfailing way—to the available stock of Reality. The truth is that I don't know what the game would have been without him. And so: *Ave atque vale, frater.*

Still the work goes on for those for whom the Mystery continues to beckon and burn. And we pick up pieces—luminous shards, really—wherever we can. In any given day, if I only pay attention, words, phrases, musical phrases, ekphrastic images, sometimes even whole poems, enter my consciousness, and I am blessed: lines sent me from Greece by a young Greek American living in the countryside north of Athens, a poem by a professor teaching in Germany or another teaching down in Mississippi. Or the wisdom of a grandchild, or lines half-comprehended in a sermon, even something picked up in the general aphasia that passes for the news each day. Or a spouse caring for a wife or husband undergoing dialysis three times a week for hours on end. Or a son at a funeral service telling us how his father, a humble man, gave away his shoes to a shoeless man down in Kingston, Jamaica, while doing service down there, joking about someone filling his shoes as he made his way to the airport and home.

These are the things worth my attention now, as they should have been decades ago, though I was too busy—as they say—to see or understand. Back in mid-September of 2017 my wife and I traveled with old friends on a bus through the Canadian Rockies, mostly among endless trees and rocks and glaciers in rain and snow. I was recovering then from several operations for brain cancer and had had a shunt placed in my head to help steady me. The thing was I was alive and getting stronger each day, and I felt—as I still do—deeply blessed to have the wife I have and the sons and grandchildren we have been gifted with. But what I kept thinking about now was this: how do I even begin to give back something in return for what I have been given?

It was raining, and it was going to rain, to echo Wallace Stevens, as we passed through the high mountains. And then suddenly, out my bus window, I saw a clearing, and then the sun was shining brilliantly against the rocky-faced mountain peaks, and then the words began coming, as in a dream, and I felt, yes, we were all on our way home, and this is what it would feel like:

On the way home

there was a moment
we were coming down
from the turbulent waters
of the Maligne it had been
raining for what seemed
hours on end there was
a thick mist hanging in the air,
a billowing high above
the larches and the pines
so that the mountain peaks
seemed all but hidden
when suddenly without warning
the face of one mountain
far off to our left began
to shine it was as if
some mystery had just revealed
the merest glimpse of what it was
I thought of Peter bartering
with Jesus on the Mount
of Transfiguration to stay, stay,
or Moses alone there on the Mountain
as the wind whispered
in all but words here I am
immerse yourself in me now,
now, for even this must pass
and you will descend, returning
to a world which will or will not
care. But know too that this moment
may well return and it will be
as if we came together then
forever and for good.[104]

For good. Home for good. As others too, over the millennia, have likewise so deeply wished for. "In His Will Is Our Peace." The very words I have etched into our gravestone.

NOTES

1 Wallace Stevens, "Of Modern Poetry," in *Parts of a World* (1942); see
  Wallace Stevens, *Collected Poetry and Prose* (New York: The Library of
  America, 1997), 218–19. All further citations from Stevens are from this
  edition and noted as *Collected Poetry and Prose*.
2 These are the closing lines of the *Paradiso* (c. XXXIII, ll. 136–45), in my
  translation.
3 "Emely," *Timing Devices: Poems* (Northampton, MA: Pennyroyal Press,
  1977), 25.
4 "Silt," *Epitaphs for the Journey: New, Selected, and Revised Poems* (Eugene, OR:
  Cascade, 2012), 145–147.
5 "East Coker," *The Poems of T. S. Eliot*, Vol. I, *Collected and Uncollected Poems*, ed.
  Christopher Ricks and Jim McCue (Baltimore: Johns Hopkins University
  Press, 2015), 191.
6 See Hopkins's commentary on the final section of the Ignatian *Spiritual
  Exercises*, Contemplation for Obtaining Love, December 8, 1881; quoted
  in Paul Mariani, *Gerard Manley Hopkins: A Life* (New York: Viking, 2008),
  275.
7 See *The Wreck of the Deutschland*, *The Collected Works of Gerard Manley Hopkins*,
  Vol. 1: *The Poetical Works of Gerard Manley Hopkins*, ed. Norman H.
  MacKenzie (Oxford: Clarendon Press, 1990), 119–128. References to
  this work are hereafter cited as *Poetical Works*, with page number.
8 Gerard Manley Hopkins to Robert Bridges (24–5 October, 1883), in *The
  Collected Works of Gerard Manley Hopkins*, Vol. II: *Correspondence 1882–1889*,
  ed. R. K. R. Thornton and Catherine Phillips (Oxford, UK: Oxford
  University Press, 2013), 619–20. Further citations from this work are
  cited as *Correspondence*, with page number.
9 Gerard Manley Hopkins to Robert Bridges (24–25 October, 1883),
  619–20. Further references, in what follows, are to this letter.
10 *Poetical Works*, 121.
11 Hopkins to Coventry Patmore (3 January 1884); see *Correspondence*, 636.
12 Hopkins's journal entry for May 18, 1870; see *The Journals and Papers
  of Gerard Manley Hopkins*, ed. Humphrey House and Graham Storey
  (London: Oxford University Press, 1959), 199.
13 See "Pied Beauty," in *Poetical Works*, Vol. I, p.144.
14 *Poetical Works*, 120.
15 *Poetical Works*, 139.
16 *Poetical Works*, 139–140.

17 "The Sea and the Skylark", *Poetical Works.*, Vol. I, 143.

18 This book is part of an extensive collection of works once held by the Hopkins family, now in the Burns Special Collections at Boston College.

19 "To seem the stranger lies my lot, my life." *Poetical Works*, 181.

20 For this citation and those that follow here, see *The Sermons and Devotional Writings of Gerard Manley Hopkins* (London: Oxford University Press, 1959), 68–75.

21 *The Sermons and Devotional Writings of Gerard Manley Hopkins*, 68–75.

22 "Felix Randal," *Poetical Works*, 165.

23 "To seem the stranger," *Poetical Works*, 181.

24 Cf. Thomas Merton, "From Faith to Wisdom," in *New Seeds of Contemplation*, Introduction by Sue Monk Kidd (New York: New Directions, 1961), 134–35.

25 "Hopkins in Ireland," in *Epitaphs for the Journey* (Eugene, OR: Cascade, 2012), 195.

26 "That Nature is a Heraclitean Fire and of the comfort of the Resurrection," *Poetical Works*, 197–98.

27 "In honour of St. Alphonsus Rodriguez," *Poetical Works*, 200.

28 Hopkins to Bridges (29 April 1889), in *Correspondence*, 989–91.

29 "To R.B." See *Poetical Works*, 204.

30 Newman's *The Idea of an University*, a series of lectures initially delivered in Ireland in 1852, would have a profound impact on the rethinking of what the soul of a university should be, a place of intellectual inquiry separated from both church and state interference.

31 *Gerard Manley Hopkins: Diaries, Journals and Notebooks*, Vol III, ed. Lesley Higgins (Oxford: Oxford University Press, 2015), 364–65.

32 Higgins, ed., *Gerard Manley Hopkins: Diaries, Journals and Notebooks*, 369.

33 Higgins, ed., *Gerard Manley Hopkins: Diaries, Journals and Notebooks*, entry for June 21; 371.

34 Higgins, ed., *Gerard Manley Hopkins: Diaries, Journals and Notebooks*, 381.

35 See "The Leaden Echo and the Golden Echo" in *Poetical Works*, 169.

36 See "The Leaden Echo and the Golden Echo" in *Poetical Works*, 171.

37 Thomas Merton, *The Seven-Storey Mountain: An Autobiography of Faith* (New York: Harcourt, 1998) 235. The quotations that follow are from the same source.

38 Merton, *The Seven-Storey Mountain*, 236–37.

39 Thomas Merton, *When the Trees Say Nothing: Writings on Nature*, ed. Kathleen Deignan (Notre Dame, IN: Sorin Books, 2015), 65–6.

40 For a detailed discussion of Berryman's life and work, see my biography: Paul Mariani, *Dream Song: The Life of John Berryman* (San Antonio, TX: Trinity University Press, 2016).

NOTES   235

41 John Berryman, *The Dream Songs* (DS 1) (New York: Farrar, Straus & Giroux, 1981), 3.

42 "The Loss of the Eurydice," *Poetical Works*, 152.

43 This anonymous poem is available online in several versions. Cf., for example, Gerald Daly of the Diocese of Westminster, England: "Sometime around the year 1600, a person, anonymous by name and occupation, picked their way quietly and unobtrusively along the lanes of north Norfolk towards the hamlet of Little Walsingham. What it was that brought them to this remote corner of the country we do not know but . . . we can be certain that they were a recusant Catholic and the thing, the place, they wanted to spy on was the ruins of the great medieval shrine at Walsingham and we know this because they left a witness in the form of a remarkable poem. . . . The writer is clearly an eyewitness of what is described and conveys an overwhelming sense of sorrow and grief at the destruction some 60 years before of the shrine under Henry VIII (the 'Prince of Walsingham' to the memory of whose name 'bitter woes' are called down)." https://rcdow.org.uk/year-of-mercy/news/a-lament-for-our-ladys-shrine-to-walsingham/.

44 John Berryman, *Collected Poems, 1937–1971* (New York: Farrar, Straus & Giroux, 1989), 134.

45 *Poetical Works*, 123.

46 Robert Lowell, *Collected Poems*, ed. Frank Bidart and David Gewanter (New York: Farrar, Strauss & Giroux, 2003), 14. All further references to Lowell's works are from this edition and cited as *Collected Poems*.

47 Two months after Hopkins's death, the poet Coventry Patmore wrote Robert Bridges that, after Hopkins had read his long poem *Sponsa Dei* in manuscript, Hopkins had told him in private and gravely that reading it had been like Patmore "telling secrets." The "authority of (Hopkins's) goodness," Patmore told Bridges, "was so great with me that I threw the manuscript . . . into the fire." This citation is noted in *Correspondence*.

48 See a letter from GMH to Richard Watson Dixon, 13–15 June 1878. See *Correspondence*, Vol. 1, 306. Hopkins was at pains to alleviate Dixon's lack of recognition for his poetry, similar to his own lack of being recognized.

49 See Berryman, *Collected Poems*, 253–54.

50 Hopkins, *Collected Poetry*, 191.

51 Hopkins, *Correspondence*, 276.

52 Hopkins to Baillie (22 May–18 June, 1880); see *Correspondence*, 395–96.

53 Hopkins to Coventry Patmore (Saturday, Easter Eve, 4 April 1885, from Dublin); see *Correspondence*, 723.

54 Hopkins to Robert Bridges (6 November 1887); see *Correspondence*, 903–4.

55 Hopkins to Bridges (19–20 October 1888); see *Correspondence*, 969–70.

56 Frances de Paravicini to Mrs. Manley Hopkins (14 June 1889); see *Correspondence*, 1003.

57 See *Laudato Si' of the Holy Father Francis: On Care for Our Common Home*. https://
w2.vatican.va/.../pdf/.../papa-francesco_20150524_enciclica-laudato-
si_en.pdf, 3.

58 See "Tom's Garland: on the Unemployed," *Poems*, 195.

59 For more detailed discussion of Stevens's life and poetical works, see my
biography: *Paul Mariani, The Whole Harmonium: The Life of Wallace Stevens*
(New York: Simon & Schuster, 2016).

60 See Mariani, *The Whole Harmonium*, 402.

61 Wallace Stevens, in *Gerard Manley Hopkins: Diaries, Journals and Notebooks*
(1937); see Stevens, *Collected Poetry and Prose*, 173.

62 *Gerard Manley Hopkins: Diaries, Journals and Notebooks*, 173–74.

63 *Gerard Manley Hopkins: Diaries, Journals and Notebooks*, 476–77.

64 *Collected Poetry and Prose*, 355–363.

65 See Stevens, *Collected Poetry and Prose*, 432–434.

66 For a full discussion of Williams, see my *William Carlos Williams: A New
World Naked* (New York: William Morrow, 1981 [and New York: Norton,
1990; San Antonio, TX: Trinity University Press, 2016]).

67 See "Dream Song 67," *The Dream Songs*, 74.

68 E. E. Cummings, "Buffalo Bill's," in *Selected Poems* (New York: Clarion,
2006), 57.

69 Eliot, "Little Gidding," V.

70 See Paul Mariani, "Berryman at Eighty: Introduction to the Second
Edition," *Dream Song: The Life of John Berryman* (Amherst, MA:
University of Massachusetts Press, 1990), xvi.

71 See "Eleven Addresses to the Lord," *John Berryman: Collected Poems
1937–1971*, ed. Charles Thornbury (New York: Farrar, Straus & Giroux,
1989), 215.

72 Thornbury, ed., *John Berryman: Collected Poems 1937–1971*, 215–216.

73 Thornbury, ed., *John Berryman: Collected Poems 1937–1971*, 221.

74 Thornbury, ed., *John Berryman: Collected Poems 1937–1971*, 221.

75 Thornbury, ed., *John Berryman: Collected Poems 1937–1971*, 223.

76 Helen Vendler, *Part of Nature, Part of Us: Modern American Poets*
(Cambridge, MA: University Press, 1980), 335.

77 Vendler, *Part of Nature, Part of Us*, 335–36.

78 See "Compline" from *Delusions, etc.*, in *Collected Poems*, 234.

79 See "Compline" from *Delusions, etc.*, in *Collected Poems*, 235.

80 Berryman, "Dream Song 4," in *The Dream Songs*, 6.

81 Percy Bysshe Shelley, The Revolt of Islam: A Poem in Twelve Cantos,
in *The Selected Poetry and Prose of Shelley: The Wordsworth Poetry Collection*
(London: Wordsworth Editions, 1994), 160.

82 Wilfred Owen, "Strange Meeting," see https://www.poetryfoundation.
org/poems/47395/strange-meeting.

83 Robert Lowell to Elizabeth Bishop (October 28, 1965), in *Words in Air: The Complete Correspondence between Elizabeth Bishop and Robert Lowell*, ed. Thomas Travisano (New York: Farrar, Straus & Giroux, 2008), 592.

84 Berryman, "Dream Song 90," Op. post., no. 13, 105.

85 See Mariani, "Baudelaire at Gamma Level," *Salvage Operations: New and Selected Poems* (New York: Norton, 1990), 120–22.

86 "The Second Coming," *The Variorum Edition of the Poems of W. B. Yeats*, ed. Peter Allt and Russell K. Alspach (New York: Macmillan, 1968), 401–2.

87 T. S. Eliot, "Little Gidding," *Collected Poems 1909–1962* (London: Faber and Faber, 1963), 214–15.

88 *Paradiso* XXXIII, ll. 99 ff. Translation by Allen Mandelbaum; see https://digitaldante.columbia.edu/dante/divine-comedy/paradiso/paradiso-33/.

89 *Paradiso*, trans. Mandelbaum, c. XXXIII, ll. 124ff.

90 Eliot, *The Waste Land*, in *Collected Poems*, 76–77.

91 Eliot, *The Waste Land*, in *Collected Poems*, 85.

92 Eliot, *The Waste Land*, in *Collected Poems*, 85.

93 Many sources quote these lines; among them, see H. W. Tilman, *The Eight Sailing/Mountain-Exploration Books* (London: Diadem Books, 1987), 581.

94 Eliot, *Collected Poems*, 77.

95 Luke 24:30–36.

96 See https://www.marygrove.edu/2006-award-winners.

97 For the full text, see Amata Miller, "Ending Extreme Poverty: The Call from Catholic Social Thought," *Integritas*, Vol 4: 3 (2014).

98 See "Dry Salvages" II, in *Four Quartets* (New York and London: Harcourt Brace Javonovich 1943).

99 Flannery O'Connor, "The River," in *Flannery O'Connor, Collected Works* (New York: The Library of America, 1988), 161.

100 O'Connor, *Collected Works*, 163.

101 O'Connor, *Collected Works*, 162.

102 Stevens, *Collected Poetry and Prose*, 316.

103 Stevens, from "The Necessary Angel," in *Collected Poetry and Prose*, 748.

104 Paul Mariani, "On the Way Home," in *Presence: A Journal of Catholic Poetry* 2 (2018), 15.

ABOUT PARACLETE PRESS

WHO WE ARE

As the publishing arm of the Community of Jesus, Paraclete Press presents a full expression of Christian belief and practice—from Catholic to Evangelical, from Protestant to Orthodox, reflecting the ecumenical charism of the Community and its dedication to sacred music, the fine arts, and the written word. We publish books, recordings, sheet music, and video/DVDs that nourish the vibrant life of the church and its people.

WHAT WE ARE DOING

BOOKS PARACLETE PRESS BOOKS show the richness and depth of what it means to be Christian. While Benedictine spirituality is at the heart of who we are and all that we do, our books reflect the Christian experience across many cultures, time periods, and houses of worship.

We have many series, including *Paraclete Essentials; Paraclete Fiction; Paraclete Poetry; Paraclete Giants;* and for children and adults, *All God's Creatures,* books about animals and faith; and *San Damiano Books,* focusing on Franciscan spirituality. Others include *Voices from the Monastery* (men and women monastics writing about living a spiritual life today), *Active Prayer,* and new for young readers: *The Pope's Cat.* We also specialize in gift books for children on the occasions of Baptism and First Communion, as well as other important times in a child's life, and books that bring creativity and liveliness to any adult spiritual life.

The MOUNT TABOR BOOKS series focuses on the arts and literature as well as liturgical worship and spirituality; it was created in conjunction with the Mount Tabor Ecumenical Centre for Art and Spirituality in Barga, Italy.

MUSIC The PARACLETE RECORDINGS label represents the internationally acclaimed choir *Gloriæ Dei Cantores,* the *Gloriæ Dei Cantores Schola,* and the other instrumental artists of the *Arts Empowering Life Foundation.*

Paraclete Press is the exclusive North American distributor for the Gregorian chant recordings from St. Peter's Abbey in Solesmes, France. Paraclete also carries all of the Solesmes chant publications for Mass and the Divine Office, as well as their academic research publications.

In addition, PARACLETE PRESS SHEET MUSIC publishes the work of today's finest composers of sacred choral music, annually reviewing over 1,000 works and releasing between 40 and 60 works for both choir and organ.

VIDEO Our video/DVDs offer spiritual help, healing, and biblical guidance for a broad range of life issues including grief and loss, marriage, forgiveness, facing death, understanding suicide, bullying, addictions, Alzheimer's, and Christian formation.

Learn more about us at our website: www.paracletepress.com or phone us toll-free at 1.800.451.5006

SCAN TO
READ
MORE

YOU MAY ALSO BE INTERESTED IN . . .

PARACLETE POETRY ANTHOLOGY: *Selected and New Poems*
Edited by Mark S. Burrows
ISBN 978-1-61261-906-4 | Trade paper | $20
"The range of poetic expression here encompasses spiritual
journaling, prayer, legends and biography, visionary and
ordinary mysticism, nature-contemplation, and, of course,
prayer, as well as formally relaxed and precise individual
poems. A worthy showcase." —*Booklist*

STILL PILGRIM
Angela Alaimo O'Donnell
ISBN 978-1-61261-864-7 | Trade paper | $18
"Poetic discipline wedded to discipleship, as handmaid to
the exigencies of love . . . all-encompassing and unified,
spiritually and poetically." —*Presence*

COMPASS OF AFFECTION
Scott Cairns
ISBN 978-1-55725-503-7 | Hardcover | $25
"Cairns's warm, calm, personal tones win him respect in
many quarters, but his core audience comes from his subject
matter: the mysteries, consolations and consequences of
Christian belief. Questions about how to live as a Christian,
how to understand such theological concepts as eros
and agape, as sacrifice and resurrection, give depth and
seriousness to his verse." —*Publishers Weekly*

THE CHANCE OF HOME
Mark S. Burrows
ISBN 978-1-61261-647-6 | Trade paper | $19
"The miracle of this collection is that out of a few 'crumbs' –
not so much as five loaves and too fishes, but the greening
blade of a crocus, a gnarly old olive tree, the chatter of
finch, the clouds that drift aimlessly by – Mark Burrows has
gathered, like a busker in the subway or Christ in a desert
place, 'enough to make a feast.'" —*Dublin Review of Books*

Available at bookstores
Paraclete Press | 1-800-451-5006
www.paracletepress.com